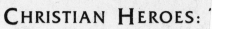

CORRIE TEN BOOM

Keeper of the Angels' Den

JANET & GEOFF BENGE

YWAM PUBLISHING

P.O. BOX 55787   SEATTLE, WA 98155

YWAM Publishing is the publishing ministry of Youth With A Mission. Youth With A Mission (YWAM) is an international missionary organization of Christians from many denominations dedicated to presenting Jesus Christ to this generation. To this end, YWAM has focused its efforts in three main areas: (1) training and equipping believers for their part in fulfilling the Great Commission (Matthew 28:19), (2) personal evangelism, and (3) mercy ministry (medical and relief work).

For a free catalog of books and materials, call (425) 771-1153 or (800) 922-2143. Visit us online at www.ywampublishing.com.

Corrie ten Boom: Keeper of the Angels' Den
Copyright © 1999 by YWAM Publishing

14 13 12 11 10   7 8 9 10 11

Published by YWAM Publishing
a ministry of Youth With A Mission
P.O. Box 55787, Seattle, WA 98155

ISBN 10: 1-57658-136-5
ISBN 13: 978-1-57658-136-0

Printed in the United States of America.

CHRISTIAN HEROES: THEN & NOW

Adoniram Judson
Amy Carmichael
Betty Greene
Brother Andrew
Cameron Townsend
Clarence Jones
Corrie ten Boom
Count Zinzendorf
C. S. Lewis
C. T. Studd
David Bussau
David Livingstone
Elisabeth Elliot
Eric Liddell
Florence Young
George Müller
Gladys Aylward
Hudson Taylor

Ida Scudder
Isobel Kuhn
Jacob DeShazer
Jim Elliot
John Wesley
John Williams
Jonathan Goforth
Lillian Trasher
Loren Cunningham
Lottie Moon
Mary Slessor
Nate Saint
Rachel Saint
Rowland Bingham
Sundar Singh
Wilfred Grenfell
William Booth
William Carey

*Unit study curriculum guides
are available for select biographies.*

*Available at your local Christian bookstore
or from YWAM Publishing / 1-800-922-2143*

Northern Europe

The Netherlands

N

North Sea

Groningen

HAARLEM
Amsterdam
Hilversum
Scheveningen

Vught

GERMANY

BELGIUM

0   20   30 miles
0   ½   1 inch
    Scale

Contents

Chapter 1

Judenhilfe!

The cold metal of the handcuffs chaffed at Corrie's wrists. Her left arm was handcuffed to her older sister Betsie, and her right arm to her father, and each of them was handcuffed to someone else. Together, the chain of handcuffed people stumbled along the alley towards Smedestraat. The morning snow had melted into gray puddles that lay on the cobblestones. With each footstep, icy water splashed onto Corrie's legs. The group's Gestapo escort barked at the prisoners in German, trying to make them move faster, an order impossible to carry out. It was well after curfew, and not a speck of light lit the street. It was all Corrie could do to keep herself and her father from losing their balance and falling. There was no way they could march at the pace their German captors wanted.

Corrie's eighty-four-year-old father simply couldn't go any faster, and neither could Corrie, who was sick with the flu. The soldiers had dragged her out of her bed, and she felt so weak that with every step she took, she had to fight the urge to give up and collapse onto the cold, wet cobblestones.

As they stepped from the alley out onto Smedestraat, Corrie wondered whether she would ever again see the Beje, the house where she had lived nearly all her life. Would she ever again mend watches in its ground floor repair shop? And would her father's cigar smoke and the delicious aroma of Betsie's fresh-baked bread ever fill the house again?

It didn't take long to reach their destination: Haarlem police headquarters. For all of Corrie's life, police headquarters had been a place of safety and protection. It was where you went for help, or to report a stray dog you had found in an alley, or to inquire about your lost purse or wallet. But now it had become a place where people were taken and never heard of again, a place of fear and betrayal where ugly, unspeakable crimes were committed. These days, residents of Haarlem avoided police headquarters at all costs. Fear and dread squeezed Corrie's stomach as the large wooden door to the building swung open and the group was herded inside.

The glare of the lights overhead stung Corrie's swollen, blackened eyes as the line of handcuffed prisoners was led down a corridor into the old gymnasium at the rear of the building. The gym floor was covered with thin mats, and small clusters of other tired, bloodied, and bruised people sat or lay on the mats. Corrie and her family were obviously not the first prisoners to be rounded up that night. Those already on the mats hardly stirred. Some just looked at the new group of prisoners as they were led into the room. It was better if the Gestapo didn't know who recognized whom.

Finally, the handcuffs were removed, and Corrie ran her hands over her battered and bruised face. The pain was still intense, but it would pass. What was important was that Corrie hadn't given up any of the information the Gestapo officer had tried to beat out of her. The secret of the "Angels' Den" was safe. For that, Corrie was thankful. A few cuts and bruises were a small price to pay for saving the lives of the six people hidden inside the secret room.

By now, Corrie longed to lie down on one of the thin mats on the floor and sleep. The flu made every joint in her body ache, her throat was raspy and sore, and her chest heaved with every breath she took. But instead of letting her collapse onto a mat, the German guards pushed her into a line of people that stretched to a single desk at the far end of the room. As minutes gave way to hours, Corrie steadied herself against the wall and wondered how much longer she could keep standing. Her body shook, both from the effects of the flu and from the shock that had finally settled over her about what was happening. She was scared, more scared than she'd ever been in her life.

Eventually she reached the front of the line. She was asked her name, age, address, names of relatives, activities she was involved in, and her movements during the past month. The questions seemed to go on and on. Even though she felt groggy and weak, Corrie knew the Gestapo interrogator behind the desk was trying to trap her into admitting something or giving up the secret of the hidden room. She prayed silently that God would help her to not say the wrong thing.

Frustrated at not being able to trap her, the interrogator finally waved her on, but Corrie stood nearby as her father was interviewed. Casper ten Boom answered each of the interrogator's questions clearly and proudly. After a few moments, a higher-ranking Gestapo officer walked over and looked at Corrie's father and then at the notes the interrogator had made. Corrie held her breath. Was something wrong?

Finally, in perfect Dutch rather than German, the officer spoke. "What is this old man doing here? The Reich does not want to baby-sit the old or the infirm; let someone else do that. You can go home, old man. Just promise you will not get mixed up in any of this underground nonsense again." There was a hint of kindness in the officer's voice.

Corrie watched as her frail father pulled himself up to his full height. Her father looked squarely into the officer's eyes and replied, "If you let me go, tomorrow morning I will open my doors again to anyone who is in need of my help. And I feel great pity for you; when you arrest a Jew, you touch the apple of God's eye."

"Judenhilfe!" All hint of kindness had vanished from the Gestapo officer's voice. Instead his cheeks were flushed with rage.

Corrie then watched as her father bowed his head slightly to the officer, as though he had been paid a compliment. And Corrie knew in her father's eyes he had. The officer had just accused Casper ten Boom, clockmaker of Barteljorisstraat, Haarlem, of being a Jew helper.

"Sit down with the others, old man," the Gestapo officer snarled.

The bells of St. Bavo Church had already chimed one o'clock in the morning of February 29, 1944, when Corrie finally got to slump down onto the mat on the floor. Corrie was huddled together with her father, her older sisters Betsie and Nollie, her brother Willem, and her nephew Peter. As she lay there, too sick, sore, and exhausted to move, Corrie wondered what would happen next. Would the nightmare that had overtaken Holland ever end? Would things ever be the same again? How she wished Holland could return to the beautiful, calm, peace-loving country it had been before the Germans invaded. Violence, misery, hatred and death had all seemed so far away then. Life did have its hardships, but those hardships seemed so unimportant compared to those they now were forced to bear. And now this final hardship could well cost the ten Boom family their lives.

Yet scared as Corrie was about what lay ahead of her, this wasn't the first time she'd faced the possibility of her death.

Chapter 2

A Very Modern Invention

"Corrie, you look hot. Come here and let me feel your forehead." Seventeen-year-old Corrie walked slowly over to her mother. She didn't want to admit it, but her mother was right. She'd been feeling sick for quite a few days now, ever since school had finished. "I think we'll have Dr. Blinker examine you this afternoon when he comes to look in on Tante* Bep," continued her mother.

Corrie nodded. Tante Bep had tuberculosis, and although there was nothing more medically that could be done for her, the doctor came once a week to visit her anyway.

The large Frisian clock in the hall struck two o'clock as Dr. Blinker arrived. The doctor hurried

---

* Aunt

up the narrow corkscrew staircase to the third floor where Tante Bep lay coughing. When he was finished, her mother asked the doctor to examine Corrie.

Corrie sat on her bed as Dr. Blinker ran his hands over her back, tapping the top of his fingers every few inches. He listened to her breath with a stethoscope, and then he tapped her back some more. Finally, he cleared his throat and asked, "How long have you felt sick?"

"For about two weeks," replied Corrie.

"And do you feel weak and dizzy, too?" the doctor inquired further.

Corrie nodded.

"Wait here," said Dr. Blinker as he hurried from the bedroom and down the stairs.

Corrie waited and wondered what might be wrong with her. Five minutes passed; she counted each minute off on her wristwatch. Then she heard footsteps on the stairs. She looked up as her mother and father entered the room. Her mother had tears running down her cheeks.

"What is it?" Corrie asked, realizing something was very wrong.

It was her father who answered. "Dr. Blinker says you are sick. You have tuberculosis, and you must stay in bed until your temperature goes down."

Corrie could feel the color draining from her face. Thoughts flooded her mind as she tried to make sense of what she'd just heard. Tuberculosis like Tante Bep? Tuberculosis, which you surely died from?

"It's not fair," she finally blurted. "I'm only seventeen; Tante Bep is an old woman."

Her mother walked over and put her arm around her youngest daughter. "I know it will be difficult, Corrie. The best thing you can do to help yourself is go to bed like the doctor said. I'll come and sit with you in a few minutes."

Corrie didn't feel sick enough to be in bed, but she needed time to think, so she pulled back the quilt and climbed in. She took her hand mirror and examined her face as she unwound her long brown hair from its bun. She didn't look very sick; her blue eyes were a little bloodshot, and she looked flushed, but not deathly ill. Not yet, anyway, she told herself grimly as she laid her head back on the pillow.

As she lay there on that summer's afternoon in 1909, Corrie tried to remember everything she'd ever heard about tuberculosis. Tante Bep was one of three of her mother's sisters who lived with them in the house everyone called the Beje (pronounced Bay-yay). She had been sick with tuberculosis for a year. It wasn't talked about much, but her mother had told Corrie that Tante Bep would die from the disease. Everyone who caught tuberculosis eventually died of it. Some rich people went to sanitariums, where they lay outside in the fresh air, and that helped a little, but as far as Corrie knew, there was no cure for tuberculosis.

The days passed. Corrie didn't feel any sicker, but she didn't feel any better, either. The doctor had left strict instructions that she wasn't to get out of bed until her temperature went down. Unfortunately, it just wouldn't seem to go down. So she kept on lying in bed.

Although her bedroom was on the third floor, Corrie had only to look at her wristwatch to know exactly what was going on in the rest of the house. Her family was as punctual as the clocks her father, Casper ten Boom, repaired.

At exactly 8:15 in the morning, Corrie's father would go down the stairs to the dining room, where two slices of bread, one brown and one white, and a cup of coffee would be waiting for him. At 8:30, when he'd finished his breakfast, he would take the huge black leather Bible off the shelf and read a chapter out loud. Then he would lead the family in morning prayer, always ending with a special prayer of blessing for Wilhelmina, queen of the Netherlands. Everyone in the house except those sick in bed were expected to be at the morning Bible reading and prayer.

After breakfast and devotions, Corrie's father would begin his workday in the clockshop. Meanwhile, Corrie's mother and her sister, Tante Anna, would start the housework. When the work started, Tante Jans, her mother's other sister who lived with them, would usually have somewhere "important" to go.

As the bells of St. Bavo Church chimed midday, lunch would be set on the huge oval table in the dining room. Once again, everyone in the house came, and often Casper ten Boom would invite one of his customers in for the meal. Dinner was served promptly at 6 P.M. Last of all, Corrie's father would read another chapter of the Bible at 9:15 in the evening before climbing the stairs at 9:30 for bed. On his way to bed, her father would always stop and pray for Corrie and kiss her goodnight. He had done so for as long as she could remember.

The first few weeks after becoming ill, Corrie had lots of visitors. She had just finished high school, and many friends came to tell her about their plans. A number of the girls were going to be nannies, and two of the boys said they were going to Leiden to train as pastors in the Dutch Reformed church. Corrie told them all she could remember about Leiden. She'd visited her older brother Willem there, two years before when he was training to be a pastor.

Her sister Nollie, who was two years older than Corrie, was training to be a schoolteacher. Each night she would come up to Corrie's room and tell her funny stories about the children she had been "practicing" on that day. Corrie's other sister, Betsie, often climbed the stairs to visit her also. Betsie was seven years older than Corrie, and she had never been well. From the time she was a little girl, she'd suffered from a blood disorder that caused her to tire easily. Sometimes after Betsie climbed the stairs to Corrie's room, Corrie thought Betsie looked sicker than she did!

Several times each day Corrie's mother would come up and visit. Often she would sit on the end of

Corrie's bed and do her embroidery and chat about what was going on downstairs.

Despite all the visitors, Corrie spent many hours alone in her bed each day. As she lay there listening, she got to know every sound in the house. It was a small house. In fact, it was two houses. The houses, which backed onto each other, had been joined together over a hundred years earlier, long before her grandfather had moved in and opened his clockshop in the front of the house on Barteljorisstraat, right in the heart of Haarlem.

Corrie's bedroom was on the top floor of the back house. Underneath was her parents' bedroom, underneath which was the dining room. A tiny room had been added on to the dining room that served as the kitchen. If the door to the stairway was left open, Corrie could hear her Tante Anna singing hymns as she made dinner in the kitchen. The front house was bigger. It had four tiny compartment rooms on the top floor. Tante Bep's room was the front compartment, which had the only window. The other three rooms had no windows because the tile roof sloped away steeply, leaving no place for a window.

On the floor beneath these rooms was Tante Jans's room. Corrie always dreaded hearing Tante Jans's footsteps on the stairway. Tante Jans was the last of her mother's sisters to arrive for a "visit," never to leave. She had been married to a minister, but he had died young, leaving her to spend the rest of her life worrying about her own death. Tante

Jans was the one who made sure the ten Boom children were wrapped up properly in case they "caught their death of cold," and she made them drink her foul-tasting mixtures when they were sick. She seldom did any housework and instead spent most of her time either writing pamphlets about how to avoid hell or visiting rich Dutch people to raise money for the many causes she was involved with. When she came up to Corrie's room to visit, she would lecture Corrie on how to prepare for death, in the process scaring her halfway there!

Corrie's favorite visitor, though, was her brother Willem. Willem sometimes came to visit on weekends, and he would bring Corrie books to read. Willem was always interested in what was happening in the world. He would save newspaper clippings for Corrie, and they would read and discuss them together. Corrie learned that American Robert Peary had succeeded in reaching the North Pole and that in Russia, Czar Nicholas was making life very difficult for the Jewish people who lived there.

The nights, though, were the most difficult time for Corrie. Everyone was asleep, and the house was silent except for the ticking of clocks. It was during these hours that Corrie would think about why God was letting her die. But hard as she tried, she could not come up with an answer. Gradually, as the weeks rolled by and summer turned into autumn, she stopped worrying about dying and decided to live each day as best she could. It wasn't long after deciding to do this, and five whole months after being sent to bed in the first place, that Corrie began to get terrible stomachaches. She thought it was an odd symptom to have, because tuberculosis makes a person's chest, not his or her stomach, sore.

Later that week, Dr. Blinker made his regular visit to the ten Boom house to check up on Tante Bep's condition, advise Tante Jans on some new medicine she had been reading about, and take Corrie's temperature. He frowned as he removed the thermometer from under her tongue and held it up to the light to read. "Corrie, your temperature has gone up. How are you feeling?" he asked kindly.

Corrie put her hand on her stomach. "I don't know if this has anything to do with my temperature, Doctor," she replied, "but my stomach hurts right here."

Dr. Blinker pressed Corrie's stomach hard right where she had pointed. "Ouch!" she exclaimed. "That hurt."

"And how about this?" asked Dr. Blinker as he pressed even harder on the other side of her stomach. Corrie curled up in pain.

Dr. Blinker asked Corrie a lot of questions, and then, finally, a huge smile lit up his face. "I think I might have made a mistake!" he said. "But a very happy mistake. If I'm not mistaken, you have appendicitis, not tuberculosis!"

Appendicitis! Never had a word sounded so good to Corrie. Appendicitis could be cured with an operation. Corrie wasn't going to die after all! And so she was rushed to the hospital, where she was operated on the next day. Within a month, she was up and about again. Her "tuberculosis" was completely cured!

Of course, after nearly six months in bed, Corrie appreciated every day. She threw herself into many projects, some of which grew to be much bigger than anything she could have imagined. Betsie taught a Bible class, which Corrie began to help with. Before long, Corrie was teaching Bible lessons at many of the local schools. And then there was the girls' club. Corrie had noticed there wasn't much for teenage girls to do in Haarlem, so she started what she called "The Walking Club." At first, just Corrie and a few of the girls from Betsie's Sunday school class would go for walks on the sand dunes before church on Sunday mornings. Then several rich people in the nearby suburb of Bloemendaal heard about the club and offered their beautiful gardens for the girls to stroll in. Before Corrie knew what was happening, three hundred girls were in the club!

Soon Corrie started other clubs to give the girls more things to do. There was the gymnastics club, the German language club, and the drama club. It wasn't long before there was at least one club meeting running every night of the week. And then in 1919, when Corrie was twenty-seven, she came up with the very modern idea of holding a club meeting where girls and boys could get together to play games and listen to music. The whole concept sounded rather scandalous to many parents, but after the club had been running for a year, most parents agreed it was a good idea.

As her clubs grew, Corrie knew she needed a better name for the club, which had grown far beyond just walking. Corrie and the girls came up with the name "The Triangle Club." The symbol on the new patch for the club was a triangle inside a circle. The sides of the triangle stood for the social, physical, and intellectual skills the girls were developing in their club activities. The circle that encompassed the triangle stood for God. At every club meeting, Corrie tried to help the girls understand a little more about God's love for them.

Once a year, the club would put on a demonstration of all they had learned, and more than a thousand people would come to see it. Indeed, Corrie's club became known throughout Holland.

Although her three aunts had died, the Beje was never empty. There was always someone who needed a home, and the ten Boom family would take them in. There were the children of missionaries who needed a home in Holland, and during the First World War, the family took in German orphans. In all, the ten Booms fostered ten children, raising many of them to adulthood.

In 1921, Corrie's mother suffered a series of strokes and died. It was a bitter blow for Corrie. Her mother had been such a help and support to her. But slowly Corrie got over the loss, and not too long afterwards she decided to become a watchmaker. Her father was one of the most skilled clockmakers in Holland, but wristwatches were becoming more and more common. Her father needed someone in the clockshop who knew how to repair wrist-watches, so Corrie went to a factory in Switzerland and learned how to make and repair wristwatches. In 1924, at thirty-two years old, she became the first woman in Holland to be certified as a watchmaker.

Soon after qualifying as a watchmaker, Corrie thought her father was going to die and leave her to keep the ten Boom clock-mending tradition alive. Casper ten Boom got hepatitis, a serious illness for anyone, but particularly so for a sixty-four-year-old man. Corrie's father lay seriously ill in the hospital for many days, until finally he began to recover. The day he came home from St. Elizabeth's Hospital was a wonderful day for the whole town.

To most of the local people, Corrie's father was known affectionately as "Haarlem's Grand Old Man." He looked like Santa Claus, and he was just as popular! The tiny workshop where he fixed clocks and watches hosted a continuous stream of people who needed advice, a kind word, or a prayer. Some of his visitors were rich Jewish merchants, others were penniless tramps. It made no difference to him who they were; he made time for all of them. So many of the shopkeepers who surrounded the Beje—the street sweepers, bargemen, flower sellers, even policemen from their headquarters around the corner on Smedestraat—had pooled their money to buy Casper ten Boom a very modern coming-home present: a radio!

Corrie cleared a space on the side table beneath the window for the radio, and when Willem arrived with it, he lowered its polished wooden case onto the table. The radio looked even bigger in the cramped parlor of the Beje than it had in the catalogue they'd ordered it from. Casper ten Boom eased himself out of his chair and hobbled over to his new, modern wonder. He ran his hand over its smooth veneer finish and declared, "It's beautiful." His bright blue eyes sparkled with delight.

"Just think," said Betsie. "We will be able to listen to concerts from all over Europe. See, I already have this week planned out."

Corrie leaned over to study the pad Betsie had been writing on. Sure enough, there in Betsie's neat, flowing handwriting was a list of which concerts were on each night, and from which station.

"We'll be able to hear news firsthand from all over Europe, too," added Willem.

From the time the four ten Boom children had been very young, their father had insisted they speak German and English as well as Dutch. This was because the Netherlands was wedged along the coastline of Europe between Germany to the east and Belgium to the south. And just a few miles to the northwest across the North Sea lay the British Isles. Now they would be able to listen not only to beautiful music but also to news from Great Britain and Germany.

The music of Brahms and Beethoven floated from the shell-shaped speaker of the radio and filled the Beje. During the next few weeks, friends and neighbors came by to see the wonderful new device. Over and over, Corrie would hear her father say, "Just think, there's a whole orchestra playing in there, and listen to how wonderful it sounds," or, "Electricity! Now electricity is amazing. First we had lights at the flick of a switch, and now machines that collect music out of the air itself."

As Corrie sat with Betsie and her father during that summer of 1924 listening to music from the radio, she could never have imagined that the radio that now brought them such beautiful music would one day bring them the news of war in Holland. And, more than that, that the parlor where they sat so peacefully and sipped coffee would become a rescue center for hundreds of desperate people and then a potential death trap for some of those Corrie loved the most.

Corrie could not have imagined any of those things then; no one in peaceful Holland could have. But these events would indeed happen, and the happy, busy life Corrie lived would be turned into a living nightmare.

Chapter 3

The Prime Minister
Is a Fool

It was May 9, 1940, and there was no need for Corrie to ask her father whether he would be staying up past his new bedtime of 8:45 P.M. It seemed just about everyone in Holland would be staying up. At 9:30 P.M. that night, the prime minister of Holland was going to make an announcement on the radio. He was going to tell the country whether or not they would be joining in the Second World War. For months there had been talk of little else in Holland. For the past seven months, war had raged all around them, ever since Nazi Germany had invaded Poland in September 1939. Since then, Germany had become even more aggressive, taking over Denmark and Norway. Many people predicted that Luxembourg, Belgium, and Holland would be the Nazis' next targets. A number of Dutch people, though, thought that was a crazy idea. They argued that Dutch people would never have to fight in a war. Throughout World War I Holland had remained neutral, supporting neither side. Why would World War II be any different? And besides, the Dutch had close ties to Germany. Queen Wilhelmina's late husband had been German, and the husband of Princess Juliana, next in line for the throne, was German, too. Other Dutch people were not so sure. They said Adolf Hitler, leader of Nazi Germany, was a madman who would not stop until he had conquered the world. So everyone in Holland nervously awaited the prime minister's announcement.

Corrie and her father knew more about what was going on in Germany than did many people in Holland because Willem had studied for his doctorate there. Although it had been thirteen years before, he had come back with a sad warning. He had even written one of his university papers on the roots of a terrible evil that was brewing in Germany. He thought that the poverty and shame of defeat that the Germans felt after World War I were a dangerous mix. He argued that the Germans were angry and bitter and as a result were looking for someone to blame for their problems. If their anger and bitterness were ever stirred up by the government, Jewish people could be in great danger. When Willem had handed his paper in, his professors laughed and congratulated him on his wonderful imagination. They assured him there was nothing to fear in Germany.

But Willem had not been able to stop thinking about the problems in Germany. He was certain they would one day spill over and infect the entire world. As early as 1933, Willem was telling his congregation about the hatred that was poisoning the German people. Whenever something didn't go well for the new German leader, Adolf Hitler, he would find someone else to blame for it. Often it was Jewish people. Indeed, in 1933, Hitler banned Jews from holding public office, from working in the civil service, and from being teachers and journalists. Many Germans, even Jewish Germans, weren't too concerned about this; there were still plenty of good jobs a Jewish person could take. However, those bans were just the beginning. By 1935, German Jews, many whose families had lived in Germany for hundreds of years, had their citizenship taken from them. They could no longer vote or marry non-Jews. By 1938, Jews were not allowed to be lawyers or doctors. Some Jews fled to America and other parts of Europe, but many others stayed in their homes, believing things could not possibly get any worse in a "civilized" country.

Willem, though, felt sure things would get worse for Jewish people in Germany. He tried to warn his congregation. Hitler was determined to breed a "master race" in Germany, which consisted of white, Christian, Northern European people. He called these people Aryans, and he wanted to "eliminate" anyone who wasn't part of this race. Of course, Jewish people couldn't be part of Hitler's master race. Neither could gypsies or people with physical or mental disabilities. In Hitler's mind, these people "infected" pure German blood and were the cause of all of Germany's problems. Getting rid of them would make Germany the greatest power on earth.

But Willem ten Boom's congregation had grown tired of his warnings, which sounded more like science fiction than fact to them. So Willem had lost his position as a local church minister. Instead, the Dutch Reformed church allowed him and his wife, Tine, to open a rest home for old people in Hilversum, about thirty miles southeast of Haarlem, on the other side of Amsterdam. The rest home housed mainly elderly Jewish people, but Willem had told Corrie that over the past four years an increasing number of young Jewish refugees from Germany had been making their way to his rest home. Each of them had a sad story to tell, and Corrie was sure that Willem wasn't repeating the worst of the stories to her. Her brother did tell her stories of Jewish people being burned out of their homes, of Jewish rabbis having their beards burned off their faces, and of Jewish children who were so scared they didn't speak for weeks after arriving in Hilversum. The stories brought tears to Corrie's eyes. Corrie wondered how anyone could hate somebody else so much to do such things to them.

A few minutes before 9:30 P.M., eighty-year-old Casper ten Boom adjusted the knobs on the big radio, which he'd had now for sixteen years and which, like him, took a few minutes to warm up. They could have listened to the speech on the smaller, more modern radio they had downstairs, but somehow Corrie sensed they all wanted to hear it on something old and solid, something that reminded them of peaceful, quiet evenings spent listening to orchestras.

The radio hummed and crackled, and Corrie leaned forward to adjust it to the station a little better. At exactly 9:30 P.M., the voice of Holland's prime minister filled the room. It sounded smooth and soothing. He assured the Dutch people that the country would never go to war. He reminded them that in the past when the rest of Europe had been at war, Holland had always remained at peace. He told the listeners that he'd spoken to both the British and the German government leaders, and no one had any intention of involving Holland in their war. Dutch people should remain calm and go about their daily business as they always did.

Corrie was listening so carefully to every word the prime minister said that she didn't notice her father climb out of his chair. Nor did she notice him walk over to the radio, where he flicked it off, right in midsentence.

Corrie and Betsie, who was also listening carefully to the speech, looked at each other. What could their father be thinking? The prime minister hadn't finished his speech yet. Without speaking, Casper ten Boom walked to the door, where he swung around to face his daughters.

"I could not listen to any more of those lies," he said angrily. "The prime minister is a fool if he thinks Holland can stay out of the war. And all who believe him are fools as well. Germany will invade Holland. We will lose. Germany will overrun us. God help all those in Holland who do not call on His name." With that he turned and headed up the stairs.

Corrie and Betsie sat in shocked silence. They had never heard their peaceful, kind father use such an angry tone of voice before. Had he really called the prime minister a fool? He never used language like that. So many times when they were children he had told them to speak well of others or not speak at all.

Finally, both Corrie and Betsie stood without saying a word and climbed the stairs, each to her own room. There was nothing to say, nothing to discuss. Most people in Holland went to bed that night with the assurance of the prime minister ringing in their ears. There would be no war in Holland. They were safe. Corrie and Betsie ten Boom went to bed with no such assurance. Deep down they knew their father was right. Holland would surely be invaded and destroyed, and there was nothing anybody could do about it.

At 2:30 A.M. that night, a loud explosion awoke Corrie. At first she didn't know what had awakened her, but within seconds there was another explosion and the glow of orange light through her curtains. She sat up and swung her feet to the floor. There was no doubt in her mind; her father was right: German bombs were falling; Holland was under attack. Corrie grabbed her robe and headed down the stairs. She passed her father's room and listened carefully. In and out, in and out, she could hear his breathing. Amazingly, he was still asleep. She grabbed the railing and ran down the stairs a few more steps to Betsie's room. Corrie found her sister sitting on the edge of her bed and rushed into her arms. The two of them clung to each other, waiting for the noise to stop, but it went on and on. Finally, after ten minutes, Betsie spoke. "Let's go into the front room and look out the window."

Corrie nodded.

Holding hands, just as they had when they were young girls, Corrie and Betsie crept into the front room. They edged their way to the window and peered out.

"They must be bombing the airport," whispered Betsie, pointing in the direction of the bursts of orange light.

Corrie nodded again, still too shocked to speak.

They stood at the window for several minutes. With each blast more orange light pulsated through the room, making the objects that had stood there for over a hundred years look strangely out of place. Finally, Betsie pulled on Corrie's arm. "Let's pray," she said, as she sank to her knees in front of the piano stool.

Corrie knelt beside her and began to pray. She prayed for the people who were being hurt or killed by the bombs that were falling, she prayed for her father, for Willem and Tine and their children, and for her sister Nollie, her husband, Flip, and their children. She also prayed for Queen Wilhelmina of the Netherlands. She even said a prayer for the prime minister. When Corrie was finished, she waited for Betsie to take her turn.

Betsie began, "God, we bring before You the German pilots up in those planes dropping bombs on us right now. We pray their eyes will be opened to the evil ways of Hitler. God bless them, and let them know You are with them always."

Corrie opened her eyes and stared at her sister as if she were a stranger. For the second time in a single night, Corrie was surprised by the actions of someone she thought she knew well. First her father had angrily turned off the radio and called the prime minister a fool, and now her sister was praying for the Germans! She closed her lips tight. She would not say anything to upset Betsie right now, but there was no way on earth she would say "amen" to such a ridiculous prayer!

The next morning, Casper ten Boom came down for breakfast at exactly 8:15, as he always did. He read a chapter from the Bible and went to work in the clockshop at nine o'clock. However, he didn't get much work done. A never-ending procession of people dropped by. Corrie and Betsie spent that day and the next four days ferrying pots of steaming coffee from the kitchen to the workshop and salesroom. Corrie carried the small radio from the dining room, where it was kept, into the salesroom. There was more news. The prime minister of Great Britain, seventy-one-year-old Neville Chamberlain, had resigned, and Winston Churchill had become the new prime minister. When Corrie heard this, she hoped that Churchill would be tougher on Hitler than Chamberlain had been. Most of all, though, she wanted to hear what the radio stations had to say about Holland. Unfortunately, the German and English stations each said the same thing: Holland was hopelessly outnumbered by German tanks and manpower, and it would be only a matter of time before German tanks rumbled across the eastern border and occupied Holland. Luxembourg and Belgium to the south were also under attack.

Some visitors to the clockshop wanted Corrie's father to pray for them; others just seemed to want to sit at the Beje, as if somehow the peace of the ten Boom home could protect them from what lay ahead. But it could not.

Five days after the prime minister had promised peace, it came, but not in the way he had intended. The Dutch put up a good fight, even though they were hopelessly outnumbered by the Germans. But May 14, 1940, became the blackest day in the history of the Netherlands. Adolf Hitler, frustrated by the way the Dutch were resisting his efforts, ordered the city of Rotterdam bombed. By the end of the day, one thousand Dutch men, women, and children

were dead, and over 78,000 were homeless. Twenty-
one churches and four hospitals were among the
buildings that lay in ruins. When Hitler threatened
to reduce the nearby city of Utrecht to rubble as
well, the Dutch prime minister signed a surrender.
The day before, Queen Wilhelmina had fled to Great
Britain aboard a British warship. In London she set
up Radio Orange (orange was the color of Dutch
royalty). Throughout the rest of the war, Radio
Orange broadcast news in Dutch every night, and
Queen Wilhelmina often spoke to the people,
encouraging them to keep fighting. When the country surrendered, many Dutch soldiers escaped to
England, where they hoped to regroup and one day
take back their homeland from the Germans.

At first nothing changed too much in Holland.
There were German soldiers on the streets and in
vehicles. Their huge truck wheels going through
the puddles formed by summer showers splashed
Corrie as she rode her bicycle to Nollie's house.
And everywhere it seemed that people were speaking German. There was also a curfew, but it was for
ten o'clock at night, and since none of the ten
Booms were ever out that late, it didn't affect them
at all. There were rules, though, which forbade
group meetings, so the Triangle Club had to stop.
And everyone was issued ration cards. The products that were available for purchase with the cards
were listed in the newspaper on Saturday. Betsie
had always been a creative cook, stretching the
food money as far as it would go, so no one at the

Beje really noticed the difference. Strangely enough, the clock business was booming. German soldiers were always in the clockshop looking for some souvenir to send home. The ten Boom clockshop sold more clocks and watches in the first year of occupation by the Germans than it ever had in a single year before.

A few weeks after the occupation of Holland began, the Germans demanded that all radios be handed in to the Dutch police, who were now firmly under the control of the German army. Corrie would have probably sent in both radios if her nephew Peter, her sister Nollie's oldest son, hadn't spoken up.

Corrie, Betsie, and Peter were sitting together in the parlor listening to Peter play a piece by Brahms on their ancient piano. When Peter was finished, Corrie sighed and patted the old radio. "I hate to have to take this down to Vroom en Dreesman's store, but I received a flier in the mail today. All radios in Haarlem are to be handed over to the Germans." Corrie sighed again and then went on, "It's been such a joy to Father, and the radio is the only way we get any real news."

Betsie nodded gloomily.

Corrie continued. "All you read in the newspapers is how wonderful the Germans are doing and how happy we should be to be a part of their great Aryan empire. I only buy the newspaper so Betsie can know what to buy with the ration cards. I never read the rest of it; I just use it to start the fire in the stove." She half laughed to herself. "Without the speeches from Prime Minister Churchill and the news from Radio Orange, how will we ever know how things are really going?"

The question hung in the air. As far as Corrie was concerned, it was unanswerable, that is, until Peter spoke up.

"But don't you see, Tante Corrie? We don't have to do what they tell us. You can keep one of the radios. Why, there must be a hundred places you could hide it in this old house!"

Amazed, Corrie turned to look at Peter. She had never thought of not doing what the Germans told her to do. But it was true. The Beje was the perfect hiding place for the small radio. Of all the houses on the Barteljorisstraat, the Beje was the most irregular, since it was actually two houses joined together. When the houses were joined, there was a five-foot difference in the level of the floors in each house. This meant there were all sorts of funny-shaped nooks and crannies around the house. When the ten Boom children were small, they had often played a game where one of them tapped on one side of a wall while one of the others had to guess what was on the other side. It was nearly impossible to know with the twists and turns of the stairs, the strange angles of the walls, and the five-foot difference between the two houses.

Corrie's imagination began to go to work. Corrie knew the Beje as well as anyone. Where was a good place to hide a radio? It would have to be easy to get to when they wanted to listen to the news.

"Let's go and look at the stairs," said Peter, interrupting her thoughts.

Betsie, Corrie, and Peter all walked slowly up and down the stairs. Corrie felt strange; she was a forty-eight-year-old woman in her own home looking for some way to trick the "enemy." Somehow it didn't seem quite real. Corrie began to giggle at the situation. Peter gave her a stern look, and she stopped.

"Here, this is the perfect hiding place," Peter announced, stopping on the stairs just outside his grandfather's room. "Look at this. It was made to hide something. I'll pull away the planks, and you can put the radio in the hollow. I'll put the planks back on top, and you can pull them away when you need to listen to the radio." Peter smiled at his plan, and then he added, "It's close to the piano, too."

Corrie didn't understand why being close to the piano was important, but Peter seemed to have thought of everything. "One of you can play the piano loudly while the others listen to the news. It will work perfectly," he explained further.

Corrie looked at her musical, teenage nephew, and she didn't feel like giggling anymore. He should be in school preparing for university, she told herself sadly, not dreaming up schemes to outwit an occupying army. Corrie felt a flash of hatred for the Germans. The intensity of it surprised her.

Later that day, Corrie carried her father's wonderful old radio off to Vroom en Dreesman's store. A Dutch policeman there copied the information from her identity card, which all Dutch people now had to carry at all times. When he'd finished copying the information, he consulted a list of addresses.

"Cornelia ten Boom, I see there are three of you living at this address. Are you sure you have only one radio between all of you?" the policeman asked.

Corrie looked him directly in the eye. "Of course. Why would we need more than one?"

The policeman grunted and waved her on. Corrie rushed home to tell Peter she had completed her first act against the invaders of her country. The Beje now had an illegal radio hidden beneath one of its stairs.

That night and every night after, a member of the family would pry open the planks in the stairway and tune the radio to the BBC in London. As they did so, someone else would beat out loud, cheerful tunes on the piano to cover up the sound of the radio. When the broadcast was over, they would all gather in the parlor for a report on how the war was going.

Unfortunately, the news was hardly ever good. By the end of June 1940, France was under German occupation, too. It seemed that Holland's main usefulness to Germany lay in its closeness to England. Of all the countries in Northern Europe, Great Britain was the only one that hadn't come under Hitler's rule. German bombers used the airports in Holland to launch air raids on London. While most Dutch people felt sorry for the English, they also reasoned that as long as the Germans' main use for Holland was a place from which to attack Great

Britain, they were reasonably safe. The German army appeared to be passing through Holland rather than trying to change it.

But Corrie had listened to all Willem had told her, and she had a feeling something awful was about to happen in her country. At first she wasn't sure what it would be, but bit by bit, the signs began to show themselves. Soon Corrie would be forced to make decisions that would forever change her life and the lives of those she loved.

Certain Guests

Like blood through a bandage, changes seeped across the border into Holland. The German soldiers who came into the clockshop weren't as polite as before. They asked questions and peered through open doorways. Slowly the comforts the Dutch people enjoyed were disappearing. They were small things, inconveniences at first. The curfew kept being moved up, until no one could be on the streets after 8:00 P.M. Each night all windows had to be blacked out with heavy drapes so that British bombers could see no lights from the air to help them work out their position.

Many of the things everyone had taken for granted disappeared from store shelves. Some things could now be purchased only on the black market, and other things not at all. Coffee became more expensive than gold, and new clothes and shoes were hard to find. Casper ten Boom could no longer afford to purchase the cigars he liked to smoke in the parlor in the evening, and Betsie cheerfully reboiled mutton bones five or six times to extract every bit of flavor from them. The store windows that were once filled with merchandise now displayed nicely wrapped empty boxes and large posters of Adolf Hitler assuring Dutch citizens that their sacrifice was going to help feed and clothe young German soldiers.

Some of the Nazis' rules, though, just made the Dutch people laugh. For example, the Nazis banned all orange-colored tulips in Holland!

But these were only minor hindrances compared to what was happening to the 115,000 Jewish people who lived in Holland. Slowly and relentlessly they were being isolated from the rest of Dutch society. Store windows had signs that read, "Voor Joden Verboden" (For Jews Forbidden). Jews were also "verboden" in public libraries and restaurants. Dutch Jews who held government jobs were all fired, and then all the "unemployed and useless" men were rounded up and sent to labor camps in eastern Holland. Already eight thousand men had been forced to leave their families, not knowing where they were going or whether they would ever be coming back. Many old and familiar Jewish businesses also suddenly shut down. One day a merchant and his family would be serving customers;

the next day the store would be shut and the merchant and his family would never be heard from again. Had they escaped from Holland, or had they been taken away to labor camps? No one knew for sure, and no one wanted to ask too many questions.

Every week it seemed the Germans made a new rule for the Jews. The Jews weren't allowed to travel without permission papers. Jewish children had to attend Jewish schools. A Jew wasn't allowed to own a bicycle, use public transport, or accept a ride in a private car. Whenever German soldiers saw Jews in the street, they mocked them. Corrie expected that from the Germans, but sadly many Dutch people were also becoming unkind to their Jewish neighbors. The Nazis formed a group in Holland called the National Socialist Bond (NSB for short), and many Dutch people were eager to join the group. Members got the best housing, the most ration coupons, and places at the head of the line when new products arrived in stores. Petrol for cars and trucks was in short supply, too, and only the German army and members of the NSB could buy it. For many Dutch people, the extra ration coupons, the housing, and the petrol seemed a fair exchange for supporting the Nazis and keeping an eye on Jewish activity. But much more scary to Corrie were those members of the NSB who truly believed what Hitler said and wanted Holland to be a part of his master race.

The war was taking some chilling turns. To everyone's surprise, in June 1941, Hitler ordered the

German army to attack the Russian army. The Russians, though, were supposed to be Germany's ally in the war! When the ten Boom family heard the news on Radio Orange of the attack, they were shocked. What kind of madman was Adolf Hitler that he would attack his allies? Like many others in Holland, they began to worry that if he could do such a thing to the Russians, what might he do to the Dutch? A strange feeling crept across Holland. No one knew whom to trust anymore or who would be the next Jewish person to disappear.

Then the Germans made a new law. Whenever they were out in public, all Jews were to wear on the front of their clothes a patch bearing a large yellow Star of David with "Jew" stamped across it. When Casper ten Boom read of this new law in the newspaper, he put on his hat and coat.

"Where are you going?" Betsie asked him as he left the house.

"You will see soon enough," he said.

He came back two hours later and laid a patch emblazoned with a yellow Star of David on the arm of his chair. "Betsie, could you sew this onto my coat, please," he asked deliberately.

Corrie and Betsie looked down at the patch, and then at each other. Corrie recognized the look of horror in her sister's eyes.

"No, father," Corrie blurted out. "It won't help for you to wear this."

Casper ten Boom looked up, his bright blue eyes shining through his rimless glasses. "If it is good enough for God's chosen people to suffer, then it is good enough for me to suffer with them."

Both of his daughters sat down beside him and began the long process of convincing their stubborn father that there were other more useful ways to help the Jews and that for now, risking his arrest was not going to help anyone.

Eventually he was persuaded and laid the patch with its yellow star lovingly in the pages of the family Bible. Although he never wore the patch, his daughters knew he would have done so proudly. He would not have had a second thought about suffering or even dying to help a Jewish person.

Sunday, May 10, 1942, was the second anniversary of Germany's bombing of Holland. Corrie, Betsie, and their father felt the need to get out of the house for a few hours, so they decided to visit Velsen, a nearby town where their nephew Peter played the organ at church.

All of the ten Booms were musical, but Peter had a special gift and had won the position of organist ahead of forty other applicants. Corrie was especially pleased about this because being an organist in Holland was an important job. She hoped it might protect Peter from being sent to Germany to work in a factory like many other young Dutch men.

After a slower than usual train ride from Haarlem, Corrie, Betsie, and their father arrived at the Dutch Reformed church in Velsen. The service had already begun, so they had to squeeze into the very back pew. Since the start of the occupation, churches all over Holland were fuller on Sundays than they had ever been. Sometimes a congregation would be so large it spilled out onto the street.

The service followed the usual pattern—an opening hymn, then a prayer, another hymn, and then the sermon, during which the pastor made some comments—not too many and not too strongly worded—about the occupation. Corrie understood perfectly why the caution. There were bound to be German spies planted in the congregation. As they stood to sing the last hymn, Corrie thought back to some of her brother Willem's sermons. It was a good thing he was no longer delivering them on Sundays. The way he spoke about the Nazis, he would have been rounded up and imprisoned a long time ago.

As the hymn finished, Corrie closed the hymnal and sat down with the rest of the congregation. But to everyone's surprise, the swell of organ music continued. Corrie gasped. Was Peter not paying attention? She hoped he would realize his mistake quickly. But he appeared not to. He kept right on playing, more loudly than before. As Corrie listened, she realized he was no longer playing the hymn. Instead, she recognized the tune of "Wilhelmus," the national anthem of Holland. Corrie put her face in her hands in horror. Everyone knew that the Germans had banned the playing and singing of the anthem months ago.

While Corrie sat worrying about Peter's being arrested and thrown in jail, she felt her father beside her rising to his feet, and then she heard his clear, strong voice pick up the tune of the anthem. As though waiting for a leader, other members of the congregation rose and joined in, until the whole congregation was on its feet. The rousing words and tune of "Wilhelmus" filled every corner of the church. It was a wonderful moment, and even Corrie was filled with pride and patriotism. But as the last refrain of the anthem faded from the pipes of the ancient organ, Corrie again worried about the price her favorite nephew would have to pay for such an act of disobedience against the Nazis.

She didn't have to wait long to find out. Three days later Peter was arrested and sent to prison in Amsterdam. Corrie cried for him as she cried for all of Holland's young men. She wondered what would happen to them all before the nightmare that had overtaken Holland had ended.

With Peter in prison, Corrie worried that the whole family was now being watched. How long would it be before Peter's father, Flip, lost his job as school principal or someone visited Willem and Tine to examine the records of the old-folks home? Willem had tried hard to disguise the fact that most of the people he looked after were Jewish, but it was difficult. Because the Dutch government had not taken seriously the threat of an attack by the Germans, it had not destroyed any official documents. When the Germans took over Holland, waiting for them were carefully detailed records of every person's political and religious beliefs. If the Germans decided to look into the records for

Willem's rest home, it would be an easy matter to find enough evidence to arrest him and take him away.

There wasn't much time in May or June to dwell on what had happened to Peter. Bad things were happening too quickly in Holland. Early in June, Willem came to visit the Beje. He seemed to have more reliable information about the Jewish situation than anyone else, but still Corrie found it hard to believe what he was telling her. Was it true the Nazis had ordered all Jews to report to be shipped off to work camps?

"What about the old and the mentally feeble? Surely the Nazis don't want them?" she asked Willem.

Willem nodded. "I think they have something other than work in mind for these people. They want to wipe Jews from the face of the earth."

Corrie closed her eyes. The Nazis had such hatred. Where did it come from, and more important, would it ever end?

Three days after Willem's warning about what lay ahead for the Jews, Mrs. Kleermaker arrived at the clockshop. It was about ten minutes before eight in the evening, and she was carrying a bag and wearing what looked like four or five sets of clothes. When Corrie first opened the door, Mrs. Kleermaker was so scared she could hardly speak. But after drinking a cup of weak coffee made from ground figs, she slowly began to disclose the details of her story.

Her husband had already been arrested several weeks before, and her son had become a diver. (*Diver* was the new Dutch word for a person who had gone underground to avoid being captured by the Nazis.) Mrs. Kleermaker herself had been in her house when she'd seen suspicious-looking Dutch soldiers standing around the front door. In a panic she had put on her warmest clothes, gathered a few special belongings, and fled out the back door. She was too scared to return home and wanted to know whether the ten Boom family could help her; she had nowhere else to turn.

She didn't need to say any more. Casper ten Boom may not have sewn the patch with the yellow Star of David onto his coat, but he, along with his daughters, was ready to help any Jewish person in need. He invited Mrs. Kleermaker to stay at the Beje until "more permanent" arrangements could be made.

Within a week, the situation repeated itself. This time there were two frightened people standing at the door. They were ushered into the dining room and calmed down with some hot coffee made from ground figs.

As Corrie poured them a second cup of coffee, she was amazed at the composure of the two people in the face of such madness. Their families had lived in Holland since the sixteenth century when the Inquisition had driven their forefathers from Spain and Portugal. Now they were being hunted down like dogs by a police force that had once been loyal to a peace-loving queen. It was as though they were all on the right stage but some people were reading from the wrong script.

Nor was there much time to dwell on how awful things had become in Holland; there were too many practical matters to be dealt with. The most important of these matters, and the one that needed immediate attention, was getting enough food. Instead of three people living at the Beje, there were now six, and because the three guests were Jewish, they didn't have ration cards. The ten Booms could not grow vegetables in a garden, because the Beje was on a busy corner in the center of town and there wasn't an inch of room for a garden anywhere around it. Somehow they would have to find another way to get enough food for them all to eat.

As Corrie thought about the problem, she realized she didn't know what to do. The only thing she could think of was to talk to Willem about the situation. She knew he was involved with the underground; perhaps he had a contact who could help. The next day she caught the train for Hilversum. As she rode along, she decided it would be best for the three "guests" to move into the country if possible. There they would be freer to move around outside. They could even help the farmers and earn their keep. Regardless of how much the Nazis asked the Dutch farmers to send to the German front, Corrie knew that the farmers would find some way to keep enough food back to feed themselves and their helpers.

When Corrie arrived at Willem's rest home, she found her brother bent over a bookkeeping ledger in his office. She walked in and shut the door deliberately behind her. "I've come to discuss a particular problem," she announced.

Willem raised his eyebrows. "What has my daring little sister been up to now?" he asked in a light-hearted voice, though Corrie could hear his concern underneath his laughter.

"We have certain guests staying at the Beje, and we are having trouble feeding them all," she said.

Willem caught on immediately. "How many are we talking about?" he asked.

"Three at the moment, but there's nothing to say there won't be three more by the time I get home," Corrie replied honestly.

Willem tapped his fingers on the desk. "I have certain contacts," he said. "I think I might be able to find homes for them, if they have ration cards."

Corrie looked at her brother in shock and blurted out, "Ration cards, of course they don't have ration cards. They're Jewish!"

Willem reached across the desk and laid his hand on Corrie's arm. "They don't have ration cards now, but they could have them by next week," he said, more as a statement than a question.

Corrie's thoughts whirled; she tried to grasp what he could possibly mean, but she couldn't.

"There are ways to get ration cards," Willem went on. "For instance, you could steal them...."

His words hung in the air.

"Could you?" Corrie finally gasped, stunned at her brother's suggestion.

"No," he replied gently. "Every move I make is watched by the soldiers. What I meant was *you*, Corrie. You could steal them."

Two hours later as she walked back down Barteljorisstraat towards the Beje, Corrie had still not recovered from the shock of her brother's suggestion. What was Willem thinking? Here she was, a fifty-year-old spinster clockmaker who'd never stolen so much as a paper clip from a bank, and she was supposed to steal ration cards from under the Germans' noses. For a moment, as she hurried down the street, she wanted to yell "No!" She didn't want her world turned upside down like this. If she were caught, she would be sent off to a labor camp for sure, and so would Betsie and her father. They were all too old and too set in their ways for such a thing.

However, by the time Corrie unlocked the side door to the Beje and let herself in, a peace had settled over her. These desperate Jewish people had come to them for refuge, and they would not be turned away. Whatever it took, wherever it led, Corrie ten Boom promised herself she would find a way to help these people.

Chapter 5

The Secret Room

Corrie tossed and turned in bed that night in her room on the top floor of the Beje. She tried to imagine herself bursting into the Food Office and demanding ration cards or else. Or else what? What else could she do? Then, as the bells of St. Bavo chimed midnight, an entirely new thought struck her. She didn't have to steal the ration cards on her own. There were many loyal Dutch men and women who would help her. Finally, she drifted off to sleep with a plan beginning to take shape in her mind. She remembered that the husband of a woman from church worked in the Food Office in Haarlem. His name was Fred Koornstra, and perhaps he could help.

The next afternoon, Corrie pushed her old bicycle out into the alley and began the short ride to the

Koornstras' house. Like all the other bikes out that afternoon, hers made a terrible clatter over the cobblestones. A year before, the Germans had made all the people in Holland hand over their bicycle tires to be shipped to Germany to help with the war effort. Corrie supposed the rubber in them had been used to make truck tires.

As she peddled hard against the wind, Corrie thought about what she was doing. She didn't know the Koornstras very well. What if they were on the Nazis' side? What if they turned Dutch underground workers in for the reward money? As she rode along, she prayed that something would happen to stop her from reaching their house if it was not safe for her to do so. Nothing happened, and soon Corrie found herself asking Fred Koornstra for help. He listened without saying much, and Corrie began to fear she'd gone too far. But as it turned out, he was thinking hard to come up with a plan. In the end, Fred Koornstra decided he would find a friend to break into the Food Office when only he and one other worker were there. His friend would tie up Fred and the other worker and steal some ration cards.

Corrie thanked Fred and waited to see what happened. The following Wednesday she heard the news. The Food Office had been broken into, and one hundred ration cards were gone. The two clerks in the office at the time had tried to fight off the robber, but they were both badly beaten and tied up.

The following day, Corrie visited Fred Koornstra to see how he was recovering from his injuries. His right eye was swollen shut, and he had a huge gash on his forehead, but he smiled when he saw Corrie. He handed her a package to "share" with her family. When Corrie got home and opened it, there were one hundred ration cards inside.

Getting enough ration cards was only the beginning of things at the Beje. Neither Corrie, Betsie, nor Casper ten Boom had given much thought to some of the other aspects of hiding people for a long period, but help was on its way.

A week after the robbery, Corrie opened the door to find a Jewish woman and her three small children standing there. She ushered them inside and showed them into the dining room, where Betsie gave each of them a cup of soup. Just as Corrie and Betsie finished seating the children on cushions placed on the dining room chairs, there was a knock at the side door. Betsie raised her eyebrows and pulled more cups from the sideboard. It was going to be a busy night.

Corrie rushed to the door. It was after curfew time now, and anyone found on their doorstep would put them all in danger. Corrie swung the door open and pulled the broad-shouldered woman standing there inside. It was only in the light of the clockshop that she realized it wasn't a woman at all, but Kik, her brother Willem's oldest son.

"What are you doing here?" asked Corrie. "Is your family all right?"

Kik nodded. "Yes, Tante Corrie, I have come to take you somewhere." And then surveying his aunt's thin dress, he added, "Put on a coat now, and follow me."

Corrie didn't dare ask questions. She knew it must be important for Kik to risk their both being out after curfew. She raced up to her room and grabbed her coat. When she came down, Kik was wrapping an old sheet around the rims of her bicycle wheels. "Not too glamorous," he said, smiling, "but it sure cuts down the noise."

Corrie nodded gratefully and followed her nephew out into the brisk evening.

It seemed like an hour before Kik slowed his pace. It was a moonless night, and of course all the streetlights were out, so Corrie had to strain her eyes to keep Kik's gray coat and green flowery scarf in view. They peddled through back alleys, over bridges, and between tall stands of trees, until finally Kik motioned for Corrie to stop. They were outside a large, stately house. Kik and Corrie got off their bikes. Then Kik reached over and pulled Corrie's bike level with his. With one hand on each bicycle, he lifted the bikes into the air and carried them up the wide stairway to the house. There was no need to ring the doorbell. The door opened at just the right moment, and Kik walked in, a bicycle in each hand, as though it were the way he visited everybody. Corrie followed close at his heels. Inside, Kik took off the woman's coat and untied the scarf. Now he looked like Kik again.

Corrie was surprised to see at least thirty bikes lined up along both sides of the elegant hallway inside the house. She wondered what kind of meeting would cause so many people to risk arrest for being out after curfew. Before she had time to think about an answer, she and Kik were ushered into the front room, where people sat in small groups, deep in serious discussion. A maid offered Corrie a cup of coffee. Corrie expected it to be brewed from the ground figs that had passed for coffee for the past eighteen months at the Beje, but she was happily mistaken. From the elegant silver coffeepot, the maid poured the strongest, blackest, richest-smelling coffee Corrie had seen in a long time. Of all the things about this strange night, Corrie would remember most the wonderful aroma of the coffee.

Kik seemed to know every person in the room, although he introduced everyone as Mr. or Mrs. "Smit." Corrie understood perfectly; the less people were able to tell the Nazis about each other, the better. Soon the thirty or so Mr. and Mrs. "Smits" in the room were all explaining to Corrie how they could help her. There was an amazing array of offers of help. A man with a bald head said he could get permission to bury the bodies of divers. A woman with thick green stockings said she knew of a midwife who would deliver babies under "difficult" conditions. A younger man offered to reconnect the Beje's telephone. The girl beside Corrie offered the services of an expert forger. Corrie tried to take in all the information, but her head was spinning. She hadn't even thought about people dying or having secret babies at the Beje. For the first time, she understood that many of these people expected the occupation to go on for many more months, even years. Clearly, she and Betsie and her father were going to have to get more serious about their "guests."

As she peddled back through the streets of Haarlem long after midnight, Corrie thought about the last conversation she'd had. A man with an enormous mustache had asked her where the guests at the Beje would hide during a raid. Corrie had to admit there was really nowhere; maybe they could climb out onto the roof and hide there. The man had shook his head and said, "That will not do. Lives depend on the right hiding place. I will send someone over to you in the next few days. His name is Smit, and he builds the best secret rooms in all of Haarlem."

The next few days flowed much as the ones before. Some guests stayed one night, some stayed one week, and some, like Meyer Mossel, whom they had renamed "Eusie," would stay till the end. Eusie had been a cantor at the synagogue in Amsterdam, and because of his Jewish looks, Willem had not been able to find anyone else who would risk taking him in. Eusie's pregnant wife Dora and their two small sons were more fortunate; a Dutch farmer and his family were looking after them.

With more Jews arriving at the Beje every day, Corrie was very glad when, a week after the midnight meeting, a "Mr. Smit" stepped into the clock-shop one morning and introduced himself as a building inspector.

Corrie greeted the little man and showed him all the precautions they had worked out so far. There was the clock advertisement in the window. Corrie explained to him that if it was ever turned upside down it was dangerous for anyone to enter. Mr. Smit thought that was a good idea. Next Corrie showed him the hiding place under the stairs where the radio was kept. He liked that, too, especially the way the hinge on the step was hidden. Then they began to discuss where to put a secret room.

The room had to be big enough for seven or eight adults to fit into, and Mr. Smit explained it should be as high up in the house as possible so the guests would have the best chance of reaching it once a soldier entered the house on the bottom floor. Corrie frowned when she heard this. Her bedroom was the highest room in the Beje, but her room was so small. How could there be enough space to add a secret room to it?

Corrie followed Mr. Smit up the spiral staircase. The higher he climbed, the more excited he got. "What an extraordinary house!" he exclaimed. "No two walls meet at right angles, no two rooms are on the same level. This is a wonderful opportunity. Here I'll do my best work." With that he flung open the door to Corrie's room.

"Ah, this is where I will work," he said with the passion of an artist. "When I'm finished, even you, dear lady, will swear there's no secret room here." He waved his arms toward the left wall of her room.

Before Corrie could say a word, Mr. Smit had shoved her bed aside, pulled a pencil and measuring tape from his pocket, and begun making sketches.

For a week Corrie slept on the couch in the parlor while Mr. Smit, the architect and builder, and Mr. Smit, the assistant, worked in her room. A steady stream of "customers" entered the Beje. One would have two or three bricks wrapped in a cloth and placed in a basket like loaves of fresh baked bread, while another would have a spirit level poked into his socks and covered by his pants. Corrie and Betsie tried to let the men work alone as much as possible. On the sixth day, Mr. Smit, the architect and builder, called them and their father to view his workmanship.

Corrie gasped, there was nothing to see! The room looked exactly as it always had. The linen closet stuck out just as far as it had before, the bookcase along the wall had the same worn-looking shelves, and the yellowed paint on the wall was peeling in places just like before. Even the molding was old and dusty.

"How did you do it?" Betsie asked.

Mr. Smit smiled. "We all have our little touches to add to the resistance," he said with a smile. Then with a flourish, he opened the door to the linen closet. He reached under the bottom shelf and pulled a handle. There was a slight grinding noise as a piece of the wall slid back. Behind it was a hole big enough to crawl through.

"If you would care to try it out," he said, looking at Corrie and Betsie.

One at a time they crawled into the space between the old wall and the new wall.

"It's amazing," said Corrie.

Betsie nodded. "I think it's wide enough for a mattress, too."

Mr. Smit stuck his head in. "As you will note, ladies, it's high enough to stand up in and wide enough for three or four people to lie down. I have loosened one of the bricks about halfway up the outside wall. It can be removed to let in fresh air."

Corrie and Betsie turned around and crawled out of the secret room.

"You should see inside it, Father," exclaimed Corrie. "I've slept in this room for years, and I can hardly believe it's in here."

Casper ten Boom smiled. "What wonderful workmanship," he complimented Mr. Smit.

"Thank you," Mr. Smit replied. "I consider it some of my finest work. You will note that bricks were used instead of wood for the wall. That way, even if the wall is thumped, it will not sound hollow. And the floorboards have been cut level with the edge of the new wall. That way, if the Gestapo ever raid the house and begin to smash the floor looking for a hiding place, they will find no floorboards running under what's supposed to be an outside wall. No, they're going to have a hard job finding this secret room."

Corrie's father nodded. No one in the Beje knew

it then, but Corrie would later learn that "Mr. Smit" was one of Europe's most famous architects.

"Now there are certain other points to discuss," continued Mr. Smit. "A secret room alone will not save anyone."

Together they climbed down the spiral staircase and settled into the dining room. Betsie made a pot of tea while Mr. Smit gave Corrie a list of pointers. First he pointed out that everything a guest has should be stored in the secret room. That way, when the alarm is given, the guests just have to worry about getting themselves into the hole. And when they do have to flee to the room, they should be careful to take with them anything they've been doing, be it needlepoint, half-written letters, even pipe ashes, anything that would alert the Gestapo to there being someone else living in the house. If they were eating, they should take their food, plates, and silverware with them, too. There would be no way to get the extra plates washed and put away in time. The secret room should also be stocked with water and vitamins at all times, and a mattress should be on the floor along with a good supply of blankets and a pot with a lid to serve as a toilet.

Corrie's mind boggled with all the details. She hoped she'd remember them all. But Mr. Smit was not finished. "The middle of the night is a favorite time for a Gestapo raid. You must practice waking each other from a dead sleep and getting to the room as quickly as possible in complete darkness.

Remember, it will be quieter at night. Everyone must wear socks only, and no talking. And one more thing—if a raid happens in the night, everyone must turn his or her mattress over. It would not do for a Gestapo officer to feel a warm spot in an empty bed, would it?"

Corrie supposed it wouldn't, but she could hardly imagine some of the young mothers and old women who had stayed with them so far flipping their mattresses over in the dark and then dragging three or four children to the secret room.

"Oh, and you need some kind of alarm system inside the house," Mr. Smit said, sipping his tea. "I will arrange for someone to set it up for you soon. And the laundry, watch the laundry. If there are clothes that don't fit any of you hanging on the line or draped near the stove...." He shook his head as his voice trailed off. Corrie understood his point.

Mr. Smit left the Beje ten minutes later. As Corrie showed him to the door, he offered one last piece of advice. "Practice the routine. It must not take more than a minute for all your guests to get from wherever they are into the secret room."

Corrie locked the door behind him and walked back to the dining room. She slumped down into a chair feeling totally exhausted. How would it ever work? Seven or eight people were supposed to disappear without a trace in sixty seconds! They would practice it as best they could, but silently she prayed they would never have to prove it in a real emergency.

Chapter 6

The Window Washer

"What possible good could it do, taking her away?" Willem asked Corrie. "She couldn't work, and it would take effort and money to transport her on one of their trains." He was referring to the ninety-one-year-old blind Jewish woman the Nazis had carried away from his rest home. Corrie stared into his tired eyes; she had no answer. So many questions in Holland were now unanswerable. Most of the time it was too painful even to ask the questions. By 1943, there were few Jews left in the country, and they were all in hiding. Those who were found were herded onto trains and shipped off to concentration camps, never to be heard from again.

By summer 1943, the Beje had six permanent guests, four of them Jewish, and a steady flow of others, mainly Dutch men trying to avoid being sent to the labor camps. Sometimes, when the situation was not too tense, Hans, one of the guests, would spend hours retyping papers and letters that told other Dutch people about the awful things happening in their country and in Germany, and laying out how they could play a part in helping to stop them. At other times, such as when Nollie was arrested for hiding a Jewish girl in her home, it was simply too dangerous to do much but lay low and wait. During those times, the men would take two-hour shifts peering out through the blackout curtain, hoping that if the Gestapo did raid their hiding place, they would be able to sound the alarm early enough and give themselves an extra thirty seconds to make a run for the "Angels' Den," the name they had given the secret room.

The days seemed to drag on and on. Of course, the guests couldn't leave the Beje, except in an emergency. Sometimes, though, they were able to sit on the roof in small groups. A thin balcony, about seven feet wide and twenty feet long, ran down the middle of the roof of the front house. The ten Booms had put up a washing line on the balcony, and many of the family chores, such as peeling potatoes and mending clothes, were done there during the day. Since the balcony was not visible from the street, the guests were able to relax a bit and enjoy the sunlight and envy the birds that flew freely around Haarlem.

The nights were more interesting than the days. Electricity was now being shut off at dusk to conserve energy for the German war effort. So many homes in Haarlem created ways to make their own lights. At the Beje, Corrie's bicycle was wheeled into the dining room after dinner and set on a stand. One after another, people took turns peddling with all their might. Of course, the bicycle didn't go anywhere, but the spinning back wheel worked the dynamo, which in turn lit the lamp on the front of the bike. As the light shone, one person would pull his or her chair close to it and perform the agreed-upon entertainment. Leendert, who had installed the alarm in the house, gave lectures on Dutch literature and organized play readings. Mary, who had been a travel agent for an Italian company in Amsterdam, gave travel talks on famous places in Italy and tried to teach everyone Italian. Even Casper ten Boom, who at eighty-four had little use for Italian, showed up for her lessons with a small black notebook and a freshly sharpened pencil. Hans taught astronomy, and then the bike would be wheeled over to the piano, where Mary would play her music. Often some of the other guests would join in with a violin or oboe. Many books were read aloud during this time. There were books of plays, poems, history, mystery, anything to pass the time and keep people's minds off the terrible things going on outside their little refuge.

But it was not easy to forget. Every person who entered the Beje could be a spy, and even a person loyal to the cause might be caught and tortured by the Gestapo for information. No one knew for sure how anyone would respond to the Gestapo's tactics. They all knew, though, that under torture, any contact could give them all up. So imaginations often ran wild, wondering whether things that seemed normal and innocent were really that way or whether they were a cover for something much more sinister.

One lunchtime in June 1943 the nine people in the house, Corrie, Betsie, their father, plus the six guests, were seated around the dining room table. Suddenly they heard a scraping noise outside, and everyone stopped eating. Corrie looked towards the window and froze. There was a man staring in at them through the flimsy lace curtains. Corrie wondered how that could be; he would have to be eight feet tall to see in that window. And so he was, with the help of a ladder! They all watched as he wet the window with a cloth and began rubbing it energetically.

"We didn't order a window washer," Corrie hissed under her breath.

Everyone sat staring, until Eusie broke the silence and whispered urgently, "Keep talking. We're having fun. We are all at Mr. ten Boom's birthday party, and in just a minute we will sing to him."

Corrie lifted the half-eaten slice of bread to her lips; her mouth felt far too dry to swallow anything, but she knew Eusie was right—they must act normal. Mary passed the salt, and Hans told a joke. They all laughed loudly at it. Then Eusie turned to Casper ten Boom and burst into the Dutch birthday song, *Lang zal hij leven* (Long shall he live). Everyone applauded enthusiastically at the end of the song, and Corrie felt it was then safe to get up from the table and talk to the window washer.

"Good day," she said as she popped her head out the door. "I didn't know we had arranged to have our windows washed today."

The window washer looked back at her with surprise. "Isn't this the Bakker house?" he asked.

"No," laughed Corrie as best she could. "I think you have the wrong address. Some friends and I are in the middle of celebrating my father's eighty-fifth birthday, so it's not a day for window washing. Won't you join us?" she asked, forcing a smile.

The window washer shook his head. "No, I'd best be on my way to the Bakkers. My apologies for disturbing you." He tipped his hat, pulled the ladder from the wall and walked off down the street.

Corrie locked the door behind her and went back to the dining room. How things had changed! Before the occupation, a window washer who had made a mistake with the address would be just that, a window washer who had made a mistake. Now he could be so much more. He could be an NSB spy or someone from the next street who wanted to earn extra rations by turning in a group of divers and their hosts. Inside the dining room, the party atmosphere had evaporated as quickly as it had come. Everyone sat silently with his or her own thoughts and worries.

And after the incident, Corrie felt safe in the dining room only when the blackout curtains were drawn. She would have liked to keep them drawn all day, but that would have certainly made the neighbors suspicious.

Christmas 1943 approached, and so did Hanuk-kah. Everyone joined in the celebration with Eusie. Each night he lit another candle on the menorah, read from the Torah, and chanted his ancient prayers.

Inside the Beje, everyone felt safe, but leaving the house was another matter. None of the guests liked the idea of going outside; every few yards on the street there was some official who might ask them for their identity papers. At the same time, they did not like being inside the Beje all the time, either. No matter how they entertained themselves, it got incredibly boring sitting inside month after month.

The youngest guest was seventeen-year-old Jop. He had been a watchmaking apprentice to Corrie and her father. After he was nearly arrested and escorted to a labor camp, his parents had asked if he could stay at the Beje. At first he felt safe work-ing downstairs in the workshop, but as time passed, he moved his work area onto a large board in the parlor.

One afternoon in January 1944, Jop and Corrie stood talking in the back of the clockshop when Rolf van Vliet, a local policeman, stepped quietly inside. Corrie gave him a friendly greeting. She knew he helped the underground whenever he could. Like so many Dutch men, he had made the painful decision to stay at his job, now under German control, and try to warn people about, if not prevent, some of the worst things the Nazis tried to do. And that was why he was in the clockshop. He had read in a police report that another underground refuge, like the Beje, was going to be raided that night. He hoped Corrie knew someone who could get a message to them.

Corrie glanced at the large Frisian clock that stood in the hallway that led from the clockshop to the dining room. It was nearly five o'clock. There was no time to send for someone in the underground, give him instructions about the raid, and have him safely deliver the warning before 6:00 P.M., the new curfew time.

"I'm sorry," Corrie told Rolf, "but I can't think of anyone at this short notice to deliver the warning. It's getting tougher every time to...." her voice was interrupted.

"Corrie, let me go. I know that area well, and I'll be fast," said Jop.

Corrie looked at the eager seventeen-year-old she had become so fond of. Jop's parents were grateful that he was safe at the Beje. How could she allow him to go on such a dangerous mission? On the other hand, how could she not let him go? He was the best hope for warning an entire "family," like the one at the Beje, that they were about to be raided. How would she feel if someone could have warned them of an impending raid but didn't?

"You'll have to be very careful," she said quickly, hoping she wouldn't regret the decision. "And we'll have to get you dressed."

Jop smiled. He had seen enough comings and goings at the Beje to know that the young men seldom went out onto the street without a dress, hat, and muff on. These days it was much safer to be a young woman than a young man in Holland, unless of course, you were stopped and asked to produce identification papers. Then the "young woman" better know how to run long and fast!

Ten minutes later, dressed and ready, Jop kissed Corrie good-bye and slipped out the side door. Corrie waited patiently for him to return. Finally, the bells of St. Bavo Church chimed six o'clock, and Corrie knew she would not be hearing from Jop until morning. Once it was curfew time, he would not risk returning to the Beje. He would find himself somewhere to hide for the night.

The next morning it was not Jop at the door, but Rolf the policeman. Rolf had bad news. When Jop had knocked on the door of the house, the supposed owner answered. Not being a regular member of the underground, Jop didn't know that the man wasn't the real owner. He gave him the warning, and then the door swung open wider to reveal two Gestapo agents with their guns drawn.

Corrie felt herself go pale. "I should never have let him go. I should never have let him put himself in danger," she whispered.

Rolf put his hand on hers. "We all do what we think is the best at the time."

Corrie nodded. She knew he was right. No one was in any more or any less danger than anyone else in Holland these days.

"I hate to say this," Rolf went on, "but no seventeen-year-old boy can keep secrets from the Gestapo. They have terrible methods...." his voice trailed off. He didn't need to say any more. Corrie knew exactly what he meant. It might take an hour or a day or a week, but in the end, Jop would tell them something about what was going on at the Beje.

Later that night, Corrie told her father and Betsie about Jop's arrest. The question, the same question the ten Booms had asked themselves at other dangerous moments, was asked again. Should they go on with their underground activities and put themselves and their guests at risk? And the answer, as it had been every other time they'd asked the question, was yes. They could do nothing else. They would do all they could to keep their guests safe, and they would trust God to do the rest.

When Corrie finally got to bed that night, she lay awake for a long time looking at the old bookshelf with the Angels' Den tucked behind it. "God," she prayed, "whatever happens, surround that hiding place with Your angels and keep any who hide there safe in Your care."

Chapter 7

The Secret Was Safe

Corrie rolled over in bed. It was no use trying to get up; she was still too sick to move. When she'd fallen asleep on Sunday night, she had hoped to wake up well enough to "work." There were ration cards to distribute, and she needed to find out what she could about where Jop was being held by the Germans. But her head was spinning, and every bone in her body ached. She sighed deeply. She would have to stay in bed for at least another day, maybe two. This was proving to be a tough flu virus to shake. It probably didn't help that her fifty-one-year-old body was exhausted from the constant stress of worrying about a Gestapo raid.

Throughout the day, Betsie ferried hot cups of tea up to her along with news of what was happening downstairs. It was a busy day at the Beje. Willem and Peter had arrived to conduct their weekly afternoon prayer meeting. After the national anthem incident in Velsen, Peter had been kept in prison in Amsterdam for two weeks, given a stern warning never to play the song again, and then released. Now he was crammed into the parlor with his uncle and twenty-five residents of Haarlem for the prayer meeting. Corrie could hear his piano playing drift up to her room as the group sang a hymn. On her next trip up with more tea, Betsie told Corrie that several members of the underground had been in and out of the clockshop exchanging information and picking up bundles of Hans's leaflets. Meanwhile, the guests were in the men's bedroom on the third floor, reading and playing chess. Most people at the prayer meeting in the parlor didn't even know there were such guests in the house.

Towards midafternoon, Betsie again appeared in Corrie's room. She opened the curtains a little to reveal a damp, dreary day outside. Earlier in the morning, it had even snowed for a while. "There is a man downstairs," she said. "He says he must see you at once. He says his name is Jan Vogel, but I've never seen him before. I said I'd get Father or Willem for him to talk to, but he insists he needs to talk to you."

Corrie swung her legs over the side of the bed and slowly stood up. "Tell him I'm coming," she sighed, as she slipped a dress over her pajamas. Sick as she felt, if the man had to see her, then he was going to have to take her the way she was, clothes over her pajamas and all. She bypassed the small mirror on the wall. She knew she looked terrible without reminding herself. Slowly she descended the stairs, clinging to the railing for support.

In the clockshop was a short man with wire-rimmed glasses. Corrie looked him up and down. Betsie was right, he was a stranger. "I am Corrie ten Boom," she introduced herself. "What can I do for you? Do you have a watch or a clock that needs to be mended?"

The short man shook his head. Without looking Corrie in the eye, he started to speak and tell about how his home had been raided while he was out. He and his wife had been hiding a Jewish girl whom the Germans had found. His wife had also been arrested, and now he had heard through the underground that the policeman holding his wife was easy to bribe. He felt sure that for six hundred guilders he could get his wife freed.

Corrie fought through the fog in her flu-muddled mind to think about what the man had said. Was it a trick, or was the man telling her the truth?

"I don't see how I can help you," she finally stammered. "I am only a watchmaker, and times are not good right now. It is all I can do to feed my sister and my old father."

The man smiled at her. "But I was told Tante Corrie would help me," he said confidently.

"And who told you that?" asked Corrie, wanting more than anything to end the conversation and climb back up the stairs to bed.

"Members of the underground. They did not

give their names; it is too dangerous of course," he said matter of factly.

Somewhere in the back of her mind, Corrie knew that the man should have used at least one of the code names when referring to people in the underground, but her head was spinning. She needed to sit down on the stool in the workroom. What should she do? The man's wife was certainly worth six hundred guilders, especially if she had been arrested for hiding a Jew. On the other hand, what if his story weren't true? Unsure as she was about the story, there was six hundred guilders in the bank, and if the story were true, it would be an honor to use the money to release a courageous woman from prison.

"Come back at five o'clock, and I will have the money for you," she said. "And now please excuse me; I am not well."

The short man adjusted his glasses on his nose, bowed slightly, and left the clockshop.

Corrie asked Betsie to arrange for someone to go to the bank and withdraw six hundred guilders, and then she climbed back upstairs, pausing outside the parlor for a moment to listen to Peter's music.

Hoping to make the most of being awake, Corrie crawled back into bed with her briefcase, which was filled with documents about the work of the underground. Tomorrow was ration card distribution day, and she had to work out how many cards each house hiding guests should get. She pulled a ledger from the bag and opened it. She wrote February 29, 1944, the following day's date, at the top of the page. She was trying so hard to focus on the job at hand she didn't even notice the date marked a leap year. Corrie looked down the list of drop-off points for the ration cards and at the number of people who needed to be fed with them. But the harder she looked, the more the numbers and names on the list became a swirling jumble of shapes. It was no use; she could concentrate on them no longer. She took her reading glasses off and let her head fall back. By the time her head touched her pillow, Corrie was fast asleep. The briefcase on the bed slipped to the floor with a thud and spilled open.

The next sound Corrie heard was an urgent cry. "Hurry, hurry. Get down. Hand me the ashtray and don't tip it." Corrie awoke with her heart beating wildly. What was happening in her room? People were racing past her bed. Suddenly her eyes opened wide, and she sat bolt upright. She was in charge of practice drills for getting into the Angels' Den, and she hadn't arranged one for today. So it could not be a practice; it had to be a raid. The Gestapo must be coming!

In an instant, Corrie was out of bed, urging people to move faster, throwing bags and pillows in after them. Mary was the last of the regulars to make it to the Angels' Den. She puffed and wheezed as the others pulled her inside. Corrie prayed a silent prayer that Mary's breathing would quiet down.

She slid the wall back in place and shut the linen closet door behind them. Just as she was pushing a basket in front of the door, a tall blond man sprinted into the room. At a glance Corrie recognized him as Arnold "Smit," an important figure in the underground. Corrie supposed he had been delivering information to the Beje and was now trapped by the raid.

Arnold looked around the small bedroom in confusion. "The others? I thought they came this way," he said in a panicked voice. Corrie flung the closet door open and reached down to slide back the wall. Arms grabbed Arnold from inside, and in an instant he, too, had disappeared into the Angels' Den. Corrie shoved the wall back in place, slammed the door shut, and raced back to bed.

She had just smoothed the covers when she saw the briefcase spilled open on the floor where it had fallen from her bed. "Oh, God," she prayed. The case was filled with information, names, addresses, and ration card numbers. If the Gestapo found it, many lives could be lost. She had to get rid of it. In a split second she was out of bed again. She grabbed the case and its spilled contents, flung open the linen-closet door, pulled back the wall, and threw it all into the secret chamber. *Hurry, hurry,* she told herself as she slid the wall back in place. *If the Gestapo walk in right now, everyone will be caught.* As soon as the wall was secure, she pushed the linen-closet door closed and made a leap back to her bed. She tried to breath normally. *I've been asleep. I'm sick.*

I don't know what's going on. I'll act surprised when the Gestapo come in, she told herself. She pushed her head back into the pillow and shut her eyes.

Seconds later, she heard footsteps on the stairs. The door to her bedroom flung open, and a man in a gray business suit walked in. It was not at all what Corrie had expected. "Who, who are you?" she stammered. "Don't come too close; I'm sick." She coughed in his direction to make her point.

The man grunted at her. "What's your name?"

"Cornelia ten Boom," she replied.

He grunted again. "Get dressed, now," he ordered, producing a sheet of paper from his jacket pocket. He scanned the paper quickly. "ten Boom, Cornelia," he read. "So you are the mastermind behind all of this?"

Corrie said nothing as she slipped her dress over her pajamas for the second time that day. Her hands were shaking so badly she couldn't get the buttons through the buttonholes.

"Where are the Jews?" the man asked harshly.

"What Jews?" asked Corrie, trying not to look in the direction of the Angels' Den. She could still hear Mary's muffled wheezing. What if the man stopped talking long enough to hear it, too? Corrie pulled her shoes on quickly and forced another cough. She had to keep coughing and get the man out of her room quickly.

She stumbled towards the door without even bending to do up her shoelaces. The man followed her, shoving her down the stairs towards the dining room. When Corrie entered the room, her father and Betsie were already there. Corrie gulped. Three underground workers were also there; they hadn't made it up to the Angels' Den in time like Arnold Smit.

The room was filled with uniformed Gestapo officers. The officer in the suit who had escorted Corrie downstairs spoke in a hard, cold voice as he pushed her across the room. "According to Herr Vogel, this one is the ringleader."

All eyes fell on Corrie.

"See what she knows," he snarled at one of the uniformed men.

The Gestapo officer grabbed Corrie roughly by her arm and pulled her out the door and down the five steps into the clockshop workroom. He threw her against the workbench, sending a tray of watch parts flying. "Tell me where you hide the Jews," he demanded.

Corrie felt her concentration leaving her; her throat was on fire; every muscle in her body ached. "God help me not to make a mistake," she prayed silently. She heard a loud crack and then felt the sting on the right side of her face. The officer had struck her. Her head smashed back against a hook in the wall.

"Where are the Jews?" he demanded again.

There was more silence, and then the crack of another blow to her face.

"How many of them are you hiding?" the officer raged.

More silence, and another blow to her face.

And so it went on. More questions, more silence, more blows.

Corrie could taste the blood as it trickled into her mouth, and she felt herself fading away. In desperation she cried out, "Jesus, help me."

The officer stopped abruptly. "Never, ever say that name in front of me again," he hissed, his steely face now red with rage. "If you are too stupid to talk, that frail old sister of yours will tell us what we need to know." With that he pulled Corrie to her feet and shoved her back up the stairs to the dining room and roughly pushed her into a chair. He smiled evilly as he grabbed Betsie by the apron and yanked her onto her feet.

Corrie sat still. Her right eye was swollen, and she could barely see out of it. Her mouth was swollen, too, and her tongue felt five times its normal size. Downstairs she could hear moans and whimpers coming from her sister. Tears stung Corrie's battered face. What lay ahead of them? She didn't want to think about it. Instead, she concentrated on the noises coming from upstairs. She could hear lots of yelling and the splintering sound of wood being smashed. She supposed they were punching holes into walls and floorboards looking for the Angels' Den. She wondered whether they could destroy that much of the house and still not find it? Corrie thought back to the way the secret room had been constructed. Brick walls so they wouldn't sound hollow like wooden ones if they were thumped. And the floor. She remembered how proud Mr. Smit had been of the floor. He had cut the floorboards so they didn't run under the wall. That way, if the Gestapo started smashing the floorboards looking for the secret room, they would not find any floorboards that ran under a supposed outside wall. Corrie breathed a prayer of thanks for Mr. Smit, who had given the guests the best possible chance. Now it was up to God to keep them safe.

Corrie's thoughts were interrupted when Betsie staggered back into the room. Her face was bloody and swollen, but she managed a weak smile as she groped her way to sit beside Corrie.

Corrie offered her a handkerchief to wipe the blood from her lip. Just then there was a knock at the side door. Corrie froze. The man in the business suit laughed with delight. "This is exactly how a raid should be," he proudly said to the other Gestapo officers. "Detain the suspects here in the home so their contacts think everything is normal. Then wait for them to come like bees to a honey pot." He rubbed his hands together, drew his gun, and headed downstairs towards the side door.

Five minutes later he was back with a young woman whom Corrie recognized as a ration card deliverer. Within minutes there was another knock at the door, and the whole scene repeated itself. This time it was a young man who was carrying a warning message that the Beje was going to be raided. He was too late, of course.

Corrie heard excited voices on the stairs, and

then two young German soldiers burst into the room carrying the once hidden radio. Corrie closed her eyes and tried to think. What else was in the house she hoped they wouldn't find? As if in answer to her question, she heard the jingle of the telephone. Corrie had taken up the young man's offer at her first underground meeting to reconnect it.

A sneer spread over the suited man's face. "Well, we are lucky for an old watchmaker and his two spinster daughters, aren't we?" he smiled mockingly. "And I thought all home telephones were disconnected three years ago." Then his tone of voice changed abruptly. "Get up and answer it," he barked, pointing the barrel of his revolver at Corrie.

As slowly as she dared, Corrie stood up and walked towards the phone in the hall, hoping it would stop ringing before she got to it. But it didn't. The officer repositioned the barrel of his gun behind Corrie's ear as she lifted the receiver. "Talk normally," he instructed in a whisper, twisting her arm behind her back. Sharp pain shot through her shoulder from his force.

"Hello, Cornelia ten Boom, watchmaker," Corrie said, hoping the person at the other end would know she hardly ever used her full name, and never on the telephone.

"You have to get everyone into hiding right away. They know who you are. You don't have much time," the voice on the other end of the phone blurted. The Gestapo man, who was listening with his ear pressed against the other side of the receiver, smiled.

No sooner had Corrie hung up the receiver than the phone rang again. The scene repeated itself, and then a third time. This time Corrie felt the caller seemed to catch on that something was wrong and hung straight up. There were no more phone calls after that. Still twisting her arm behind her back, the gray-suited man directed Corrie back to the others. As Corrie sat down in the dining room, a parade of people were led down the stairs. Corrie could see each one through the open door. She knew most of them from Willem's prayer meeting. She felt sorry for them—the retired missionary from the Dutch East Indies, the woman from the bakery down the street—they knew nothing about the guests at the Beje. Corrie's heart dropped when Willem and Peter passed the door. And then she gasped out loud when she saw Nollie trailing behind them. What had she been doing at the Beje? Nollie had already been arrested once for sheltering a Jewish girl. She had been released, but the Germans wouldn't be so easy on her this time. Tears sprung to Corrie's eyes. All four ten Boom siblings had been captured by the Gestapo, and so had one of Corrie's nephews.

Just then there was a yell of triumph from upstairs. Corrie looked at Betsie, the terror in her eyes confirming that they were thinking the same thing. The Angels' Den! They must have found it.

Corrie could hear the shouts in German. "Come and see what I've found! Innocent watchmakers, ha!" Corrie held her breath, waiting to hear some noise to confirm the discovery of the room.

Buzz buzz. It was the alarm Lenert had installed for them. It was sounding all over the house. A minute or so later, the man in the gray business suit strolled back into the dining room. "A very efficient alarm system," he said. "And I have to ask myself what a family like you might need an alarm for." He looked at Corrie questioningly.

Corrie shook her head, giddy with joy. Finding the alarm system would make things harder for her, Betsie, and their father with the Gestapo, but at least they hadn't found the secret room. Corrie looked at the man defiantly through her unswollen eye. She hoped the message was clear; the Gestapo could beat her as much as they wanted, but they would not get any information from her.

The man must have understood. He swung around abruptly and yelled at the group, "Get up, and follow them," pointing towards the two Gestapo officers at the door. "We've got quite a little haul here," he taunted Corrie as she staggered to her feet. "You could have made it easier for everyone by telling us where your precious Jews are hidden. But don't worry, we'll put a twenty-four hour guard on this place. Either they'll die like cowards and we'll smell their rotting bodies in the end, or they'll come crawling out of the woodwork like cockroaches in a couple of days. You would have done them a favor by telling us where they are," he said with a cruel smile.

Corrie reached for the wall to steady herself before walking defiantly past the man. Her face might be battered and bruised, but she was the one who still held the secret to the location of the Angels' Den. And as long as she held onto that secret, she hoped and prayed that the guests huddled inside it would be safe.

Chapter 8

A Privileged Family

The Frisian clock in the hallway struck eleven o'clock as the group from the dining room marched past. It had been eight hours since the Gestapo had raided the Beje. Casper ten Boom broke rank and walked over to the clock. He opened its glass door and reset the weights. "It would not do to let the clock run down," he said, as he reached for his hat. Corrie put her arm around him as they walked out of the Beje. Outside they were herded together with the people who had been attending the prayer meeting and were hand-cuffed together to form a long chain. Corrie was linked at the wrist to her father on her right and to Betsie on her left. As she stood in the cold, dark alley, a hundred images raced through her mind.

She thought of playing hoops with Nollie, of waiting for the streetcar to stop outside the clockshop and deliver Tante Jans back from one of her meetings, of the foster children organizing running races from one end of the alley to the other, of Kik waiting silently at the side door to escort a guest to safety. And then there was the horror of the present. Corrie was the captive of an army that had invaded her peaceful country. And now that invading army stood ready to tear her family and world apart.

One of the Gestapo officers barked an order for them all to march, and they began to make their way along the alley towards Smedestraat and the Haarlem police headquarters. It took only a few minutes to reach the headquarters, but it took more than two hours to be processed. Finally, well after 1:00 A.M., Corrie got to lie down on a thin mat on the floor of the gymnasium at the back of police headquarters. The gym had been turned into a large holding cell for all the people the Germans had rounded up that day. Corrie felt so wretchedly ill she didn't care that the mat was lumpy and the cold wooden floor beneath was hard; she was just glad to be lying down again at long last.

The Gestapo had wanted to let Casper ten Boom go, but he refused to agree to their demand not to shelter any more Jews. So now he, Corrie, Betsie, Nollie, Willem, and Peter all huddled together on the mats on the floor. None of them knew what lay ahead. Casper ten Boom, seeing the concern on the faces of his children and grandson, spoke up.

"Never, forget," he said, his blue eyes shining, "what a privileged family we are." Corrie felt tears cascade down her swollen face as he spoke. *God, help me to never forget those words*, she prayed silently.

Through the rest of the long night, Corrie tossed and turned on her thin strip of gym mat. She prayed for those left behind in the Angels' Den. She asked God to somehow keep them all safe.

Slowly the pale morning sun filtered through the high windows of the gymnasium. People lying on the mats around the large room began to stir. Baskets of soft white bread rolls were handed around by the Dutch policemen. Corrie caught sight of Rolf van Vliet. He nodded slightly at her. She knew there was little he could do for them now. Corrie tried to force down a piece of bread; it could be the last food she would have for a long time, but her lips were still too swollen and sore to bite and chew. She still felt feverish from the flu. After about fifteen minutes, German soldiers marched into the gym. An officer yelled for the prisoners to form a line and march outside to a waiting bus. Corrie and Betsie reached for their father and pulled him up from the mattress. He seemed older and more frail than ever after his night in the crowded gym. Corrie wondered how long he would survive in such conditions.

As they walked out of the Haarlem police head-quarters, Corrie was shocked to see a hundred or more people lined up along the sidewalk. It was a risk for them to even be out on the sidewalk in such a group. Corrie knew that they had come, regardless of the personal risk, to show their support for the residents of Haarlem whom the Nazis had arrested for doing nothing more than offering kindness and protection to innocent human beings who were being hunted down like wild animals.

The prisoners stood in the bus as it wound its way through the streets of Haarlem. Corrie stared out the window, trying to fix the beauty of the spring tulips and pink plum blossoms in her memory.

After the bus had rumbled along for a while, it came to a halt. The prisoners were herded off and loaded onto large trucks with canvas canopies on the back. Corrie hoped and prayed that they were not being taken to Germany. She breathed a sigh of relief when one of the other prisoners, a man with a bandaged hand, pointed out that they were headed west towards the coast. "They're taking us to the prison at Scheveningen," the man predicted. He was right.

After more than an hour rolling through the countryside, the truck lurched to an abrupt stop. The sides of the canvas canopy were unlaced and thrown open. Then the yelling began. Corrie wondered why every German occupying Holland had to yell so loudly. Her head was already throbbing from the effects of the flu, and the last thing she needed was someone yelling in her ear. She climbed down from the truck.

"Quickly, noses against the wall. Now!" yelled one of the German soldiers, pointing to the high concrete wall that surrounded the prison courtyard.

The crowd surged toward the wall, carrying Corrie along with it. Corrie found herself facing the concrete wall, glad to have something to lean against. Slowly, so as not to draw attention to herself, she turned her head from one side to the other. She spotted Willem, Nollie, and Betsie to her right, but she could not see Peter and her father anywhere. She felt panic rising in her. Anything seemed bearable as long as she could stay with her family.

Corrie dared not look down at her watch, but she figured they had all been standing with their noses against the wall for about an hour and a half. She was so weak from the flu, it was amazing she'd been able to stay standing for so long. Finally, from behind, someone barked instructions. "Female prisoners, to the right. Follow me."

Corrie turned around quickly, hoping it would give her time to scan the group for her father and Peter. Betsie and Nollie jostled their way over until the three sisters were moving together. Corrie spotted Peter standing farther along the wall but could not see her father. She kept searching for him as the crowd of women moved towards a door to the right. Finally, her shoulders relaxed; there he was. Casper ten Boom was the only person in the courtyard sitting on a chair. Corrie marveled at how peaceful he looked. It was as if he were sitting in his favorite chair at the Beje, smoking a cigar and listening to a concert on the radio. On an impulse, Corrie yelled, "Father, God go with you!" Her voice echoed through the courtyard.

Casper ten Boom turned his head and smiled. "And with you, too, my daughters," he called back. It was the last time Corrie, Betsie, and Nollie were to see their father.

Corrie grabbed Betsie's arm, and they stepped in line to follow the other women. Corrie's heart thumped loudly in her chest. She wondered whether she would be punished for yelling in the courtyard. If she was punished, it would be worth it to have heard her father's voice one more time.

The metal doors clanged shut behind them. The women were all in a wide hall with a concrete floor. Along the middle of the floor ran a strip of seagrass matting. Corrie stepped onto it, grateful to have a little cushioning under her feet.

"Off the mat, now!" yelled the guard. "Prisoners are not permitted to step on the mat."

Corrie and a group of other "offenders" stepped back onto the concrete. Corrie wondered how many other stupid rules the prison had. The women waited in a long line while their personal information was taken one more time and they were stripped of their personal belongings. Corrie took off her watch and her mother's wedding ring and dropped them into a manila envelope. She was certain she would never see them again. Once all of the women had been processed this way, a female guard yelled for them to follow her. She picked up a clipboard, and they all headed down the hall. On each side were thick metal doors with numbers on them. The guard halted outside the first door and read a name from the list. It was one of the members of the prayer group. The woman staggered forward, a shocked expression on her face. Corrie felt sorry for her; less than twenty-four hours ago the woman had been an innocent participant in a prayer meeting above a clockshop. Now she was about to be locked up in a prison cell.

The guard produced a huge set of keys from her pocket, located the right one, and unlocked the cell door. Corrie stopped coughing long enough to crane her neck for a look inside. The cell was no larger than a full-sized bed, and three women were already in it. The guard pushed the woman inside and slammed the metal door shut. The sorry procession continued on. Only one woman was dropped off at any cell, never two or three together. Corrie's heart sank. She guessed it was deliberately done so that no two women from Haarlem were together. Unless there was a miracle, she and her two older sisters would soon be separated.

And so they were. First Betsie was deposited in a cell, and then Nollie. She squeezed Corrie's hand one last time before being pushed into a cell.

There were only three women left in the line when Corrie's name was finally called. Corrie coughed and stepped into the cell. The guard yelled in after her, "Get off that bed and give it to this one; she's sick." Corrie stood with her back against the wall and adjusted her eyes to the light of a single bulb. Running along the right side of the wall was one narrow cot with a thin mattress covering it. On the floor beside it were three straw-filled pallets. Spread out as they were, the pallets took up the entire cell floor. Under the cot was a metal bucket with a lid and basin containing gray water.

"Sick! Don't come near me if you're sick!" screeched the old woman in a tattered green dress who was lying on the bed. "We're going to die in here soon enough without your diseases."

Corrie kept standing with her back against the door. She had no energy, and unless someone made room for her, there was nowhere else to go.

"Come on, frau," she heard the young woman on the floor say to the woman on the bed. "I'm sure she's not that sick."

As if to contradict her, Corrie had a coughing fit. She could hear her chest gurgling, and she couldn't catch her breath. Eventually the coughing stopped, and begrudgingly the older woman rolled off the cot and onto the floor with the other two women.

"I'm so sorry," Corrie tried to apologize, but the younger woman stopped her.

"That's all right," she said soothingly. "Welcome to our cell."

Corrie smiled weakly as she lay down. A billow of dust rose from the mattress along with the stench of urine. Corrie gagged and rolled onto her back. Slowly her eyes grew heavier and heavier until she fell asleep.

Clang! Clang! Corrie awoke with a start. Where was she? What was that noise?

"Hurry up," urged a voice from below her. "Pick

up your plate off the shelf or you won't get any food."

Corrie took a deep breath, and the memories of the night before came flooding back to her.

The older woman in the green dress pointed towards the door. Corrie crawled to the end of the cot and reached down. A small flap had been unlatched in the front of the door, and four plates of gruel were balanced on it. Corrie took the last plate and set it on her knees. She looked at it for a long time. It was a watery gray color with specks of something brown floating in it. She bent her head down to smell it and recoiled. Quickly she handed it to the woman in the green dress who had already gobbled hers down. "Here, eat this," she said, "there's no way I could."

"Wanna bet?" said the old woman. "They all say that when they come here, but after a day or two, they're gulping it down just like the rest of us. You'll see."

The woman was right. By the time the gruel arrived the following morning, Corrie was ready to eat it.

There were no windows in the cell, so the days were counted by the arrival of the food each morning. From there the day followed a dull routine. Around midday, the metal flap in the door was swung open again, and four slices of brown bread appeared. About an hour later, a key rattled in the lock, and the door was cracked open. One of the women handed out the toilet bucket, which sometimes had overflowed onto the pallets. The dirty water basin was also handed out and came back with fresh water. The toilet bucket was returned empty, along with two squares of toilet paper each.

Inside the cell, the women tried to be as polite to each other as possible, but each one was living her own personal nightmare. The youngest girl, who had spoken kindly to Corrie the night before, told her she was a baroness whose father had refused to serve in the German navy. She spent many hours each day pacing up and down the cell, six steps turn, six steps turn. She hardly ever sat down, and when she did, she would put her hands over her face and weep.

The old woman in the tattered green dress announced she was a cleaning woman who had not reported that a Jewish boy was living in a house she cleaned. She told the Gestapo she hadn't known he was there, but it had made no difference.

The third woman spent hours at a time sitting with her right ear on the metal door.

"What is she doing?" Corrie asked the old woman in the green dress.

"Information," she replied.

Corrie looked puzzled.

"She knows what every sound means in this hellhole," the old woman went on. "She can tell you if it's the matron walking past or a guard. She can even tell you which cell they stop at and how many people they take away. She gets it dead right every time. It's uncanny."

As if to prove the point, the third woman, still with her ear to the door, whispered, "Someone in 316 is being led away by a guard. They're headed towards the west wing. Third time this week. I wonder what's up?"

"Amazing," said Corrie with genuine admiration. She herself was good at listening. Sometimes when a watch was not working right, she would listen to it carefully for a minute or two to see whether she could hear the problem. But this woman was truly remarkable in her listening abilities. "How long have you been here?" Corrie asked her.

"Three years, maybe a bit longer," was the reply.

Corrie's heart sank. Three years! The Germans would keep a person locked up for three years without seeing sunshine or feeling the wind, and without a bath or a book to read! "Poor father! Poor Betsie!" Corrie groaned as she sat wearily on the edge of the cot. She wondered how long she would be locked in the cell.

Chapter 9

The Clocks at the Beje Are Safe

A key rattled in the lock of the cell door. The door swung open, and the prison matron stepped into the cell. "ten Boom, Cornelia," she bellowed as if there were forty prisoners in the cell, not four.

Corrie struggled into a sitting position on her cot. Every joint in her body ached, and every breath she drew was an effort.

"Get up. Bring your hat and coat and follow me," the matron directed and stepped outside the cell to wait.

Corrie set her feet on the floor and stood up cautiously. She was still wearing her coat; it had been too cold to take it off since arriving in the cell three days earlier.

"A hat," whispered the woman with remarkable

107

hearing, still seated near the door. "A hat can be good or bad. It means you are leaving the building."

As usual, the woman was right. Corrie was led down the hallway, out the door, and into a waiting car. She sank into the leather back seat of the car where several other prisoners were also seated. As they drove off, Corrie stared hungrily out the window. Had the sky always been such a brilliant blue? Had the clouds always danced across the sky like that? Fresh air streamed into the car, and Corrie breathed deeply to fill her lungs with it. And better, it was sea air with a delightful salty smell.

The car glided through the prison gates and out into the streets of Scheveningen. There were people everywhere in the streets: people walking, people standing on street corners talking, people walking their dogs, and children skipping. Corrie could hardly believe it was real. Did these people have any idea how blessed they were? They were free. Free to bathe and clean their teeth and read books and listen to music.

Corrie was so engrossed looking out the window she hardly noticed when the car slowed and finally stopped outside a large brick building. The passengers were told to get out and follow a guard up the steps into the building. One of the passengers was too sick to walk any farther, and to Corrie's surprise, an orderly appeared with a wheelchair for him.

Several minutes later, Corrie found herself in a large waiting room with rows of wooden chairs.

After an hour of sitting and waiting, she had to use the bathroom. She told a guard, who called the nurse seated at the desk in the corner. The nurse took Corrie's arm and led her down the corridor. Instead of waiting outside the toilet cubicle, the nurse followed Corrie in and shut the door after them. "What can I get for you?" she whispered urgently.

Corrie was stunned by her kindness. These days she wasn't used to anyone in a uniform being friendly towards her. Her mind reeled with possibilities, but one thing was more important than any other. "A Bible. Can you get me a Bible?" she asked.

The nurse smiled. "I'll try," she said, and then she quickly unlocked the door and waited outside for Corrie. On the way back to the waiting room, neither of them spoke.

It was another hour before Corrie's name was finally called, and Corrie entered a side room for a medical examination. The doctor felt her pulse, took her temperature, and listened to her lungs and heart with a stethoscope. "Hum," he said, scribbling something on his pad. "Pleurisy. Normally I would tell you to get plenty of rest and keep warm, but under these circumstances...." His voice trailed off as he shrugged his shoulders.

Corrie stood and walked to the door. The doctor followed her. In a low voice he said, "Good-bye and good luck. I hope I have done you a favor reporting your pleurisy."

As Corrie walked back to her seat, the nurse brushed past her, and Corrie felt a small package being pressed into her hands. She slid it into her coat pocket and kept walking toward her seat. Soon afterwards, the prisoners were led back to the car. As they were ferried through the streets of Scheveningen back to the prison, Corrie had two things on her mind: the package in her coat pocket and the doctor's words. She rested her hand lightly on the outside of her coat pocket while she wondered whether the doctor had really done her a favor. Would having pleurisy be a good thing? Would the Germans possibly let her go? Or would they transfer her to a hospital? Corrie desperately hoped they would, but she also knew that the Nazis had little patience with the sick and the old, and to them she was both.

"You're back," three voices rang out as Corrie was led back into the cell. "What happened? Where did they take you? Did you hear anything about the war?" they all asked at once.

Corrie sat on the edge of the cot and told them everything. When she got to the part about the package, she drew it from her pocket. Everyone gasped. "Open it, open it," they urged, like little children at a birthday party. Corrie tore open the newspaper the package was wrapped in and removed the contents one at a time. There were two small bars of soap, real soap like the kind you could buy in stores before the war. She passed them around, and everyone sniffed the soap's fresh, flowery scent. Next Corrie produced a chain of about ten safety pins. They, too, were passed around and admired as though they were a diamond necklace. At the bottom of the package was the best thing of all: four small booklets. Corrie lifted them up and kissed them; they were booklets of the four Gospels. She offered one to the old woman in the green dress. The woman recoiled. "Don't touch them," she said with horror in her voice.

"It's the Bible," said Corrie, thinking she didn't understand.

"I can see that," the old woman snapped. "Do you want to get us all in trouble? Get caught with a Bible and you get your sentence doubled plus *kalte kost* for the rest of your stay."

Kalte kost was a dreaded word in the prison; it referred to bread and water rations with no hot food. The threat of kalte kost hung over each prisoner in his or her cell just as surely as the single lightbulb did. A prisoner got kalte kost for talking too loudly, for singing, for spilling the toilet bucket, for asking guards questions, for walking on the seagrass mat. The list went on and on.

Corrie laid the four Gospels on her mattress. "Kalte kost would be a small price to pay for these," she said.

The other women stared blankly at her.

That night Corrie lay on her thin mattress reading the Gospel of John. She could hear her father's voice echoing in her mind as she read. She thought about him reading aloud from the Bible to the family each morning and evening. She wondered how he was. She also wondered about the guests in the

Angels' Den back at the Beje. Was it possible they were safe, even with the Gestapo guarding the house? And then her mind wandered again to the doctor's words earlier in the day: "I hope I've done the right thing reporting your pleurisy." Had he?

Corrie didn't have to wait long to find out. Two nights later the key rattled in the lock of the cell door. It was the prison matron again. "ten Boom, Cornelia, get up and bring your things. No talking," she barked.

Secretly, Corrie slipped the four gospel booklets into her coat pocket, pulled her hat from the peg, and followed the matron. This time, though, they did not turn right to head down the hallway, but they turned left. Corrie's heart sank. They were headed farther inside the prison. About five hundred feet along the hallway, the matron stopped, found another key on her ring, and opened a cell door. Without even needing to be told, Corrie stepped inside. The layout of the cell was the same as the one she had just left, but the cell was different in two ways. There were no other prisoners in the cell, and the cell had a window. The window was high up on the wall and covered with bars, but it was a window nonetheless. In this cell, Corrie would have fresh air and sunlight. She decided she would drag her cot over to the outside wall in the morning and climb up and look out the window. Before she went to sleep, Corrie scratched a mark on the wall beside her cot and wrote the date, March 6, 1944. Somehow, she felt it was important not to lose track of time.

The next morning Corrie was so weak she was unable to stand up at all. She lay on the cot and looked at the sky through the twenty-eight tiny squares the bars formed across the window. Mealtime came, and a guard peered in through the food slot. Corrie waved her hand slightly. The guard grunted and flung the slice of bread at her through the small opening. The bread landed near the cot, and Corrie picked it up from the filthy floor and hungrily gulped it down. Then she waited, wondering what would happen next. An hour or so later, a trolley squeaked down the hallway and stopped outside her cell door. It was a medical attendant with foul-tasting medicine for Corrie to take. The attendant was wearing a prisoner's uniform, and Corrie knew she was what the other prisoners referred to as a "trusty," a fellow prisoner who got to help run some of the things in the prison. Trusties cooked the soup, swept the floors, and dispensed medicine. In return they were given extra privileges by the guards. Corrie felt sure the trusty would know a lot about what was going on in the prison.

After swallowing the wretched medicine, Corrie begged of the trusty, "Have you heard anything of the ten Booms or the van Woerdens?"

"Save your breath, woman," snarled the trusty. "You don't think I can talk to you and keep my job do you?" She glared at Corrie and then slammed the cell door shut.

Corrie lay down again on the cot. "So prison is just like the outside," she said aloud to herself.

"There are prisoners in here who will take risks to help each other and prisoners who won't."

Each day the trusty came to her cell with the awful medicine, but she never said another word to Corrie. The medicine she brought, though, seemed to be working, and slowly Corrie began to feel better. Even so, no other prisoners were put in the cell with her. As the long, boring weeks rolled by, Corrie became very lonely. One day as she scratched another mark on the wall, she noticed it was April 15. It was her fifty-second birthday. She tried to sing a song to remind herself of the many happy birthdays she'd had at the Beje, but the guard banged on the cell door and yelled, "Prisoners are not permitted to sing. Shut up or kalte kost." So she sang the song in her head.

Hardly a minute went by that Corrie didn't think about her father and her family. She desperately wanted to know whether they were all right. Her answer came partly as the result of another birthday. Only five days after her own, on April 20, Adolf Hitler turned fifty-five years of age. The guards all went to a party to celebrate his birthday and left the cells unguarded. There was no thought of anyone's escaping; the doors were all locked, and the prisoners were fed so little that most of them could not have staggered far anyway. But the absence of the guards meant that the prisoners could yell to each other. At first, Corrie was confused by all the yelling, but gradually the noise died down, and the prisoners organized themselves. Up and down the hallway from cell to cell they took turns yelling and listening back and forth.

Corrie was delighted to yell messages to the prisoners in the next cells to hers. "Tell Ruud Engers that Hetty was released in February." "To Rosina Kaufman, your mother is in cell 463; she is well and sends her love." Some of the messages, though, were sad, and it was hard to pass them on. "To Isaac Franken, they took our twins. Have you heard where they are? From your wife Gertrude." "To Joel Kugler, your brother Fritz was sent to a labor camp last week."

To this stream of messages Corrie added her own. "I am Corrie ten Boom in cell 384. Is there any news of Casper, Willem, and Betsie ten Boom and Nollie and Peter van Woerden?"

She listened closely as the message echoed down the empty corridor. More messages flowed back and forth. Corrie waited and waited. Finally an answer came. "Willem ten Boom and Peter van Woerden were released." Corrie clapped her hands and laughed with joy.

Then there was another message. "Nollie van Woerden released." Corrie's hopes soared. Maybe all the other members of her family had been freed! But the next message told her otherwise: "Betsie ten Boom in cell 314 says to tell her sister God is good." How like Betsie. No matter how hard things were, she trusted God.

The stream of information continued. There were rumors about the war. The British air force had bombed the Public Records Building in The Hague, destroying many important Nazi records, and the Americans were making progress against the Japanese in the Pacific. Then finally, the clamor of voices began to die down until the prison was silent again.

Corrie sat on her cot and thought about the messages she had heard. It seemed everyone arrested at the Beje had been released except for Betsie and her. But what about her father? It was strange no one had any word of him; he was so old and distinguished looking with his long white beard, it would be hard to forget him. Corrie tried not to think the worst.

Two and a half weeks later on May 3, Corrie found out why she had not heard about her father. A letter was dropped through the food slot. Corrie stared at it. She had waited so long for news from home, and now that it was lying on the floor in front of her, she was too scared to pick it up. Finally, she got up the courage and reached down and picked up the letter. It was from Nollie. Corrie tore it open. It did not start out well. "Dear Corrie," it read. "I need you to be very brave. The news I have to tell you is not going to be easy to read...." Corrie's eyes welled with tears, but she wiped them away and kept reading. "Father was in prison for only ten days; then his soul was released, and he went to be with the Lord."

Corrie burst into loud sobs. Her father, her dear, dear, wonderful father had died in this dirty prison surrounded by so much hatred and violence. Corrie could hardly bear to think about it. She could not be at his funeral, and she couldn't be with her family. It was so unfair, and she sobbed louder. After many minutes of sobbing, she thought about the time her father had wanted to wear the yellow Star of David on his coat to identify with the Dutch Jews. When Corrie and Betsie had tried to stop him, he had told them, "If it is good enough for God's chosen people to suffer, then it is good enough for me to suffer with them." As Corrie thought about those words, she began to feel calmer. Her father had died for something he believed in, and he wouldn't have had it any other way.

The next morning Corrie reread the letter. As she did so, she noticed that the writing on the envelope was very sloped, while the writing in the letter was not. What could it mean? Was there a reason Nollie had done that? Suddenly she remembered a letter that had come to the Beje for her nephew Kik. Kik had soaked off the stamp, underneath which was an important message from the underground. With trembling hands, Corrie put the envelope into the basin of water. Sure enough, when the stamp had soaked off, she could see tiny writing. She held the envelope up to the light and read. "All the clocks at the Beje are safe." It was a code, but Corrie knew exactly what it meant. She broke into sobs once again. This time they were sobs of joy. Somehow all of the guests in the Angels' Den had made it to safety. For the first time since being arrested, Corrie felt something inside other than fear and dread.

Chapter 10

The Reading

Corrie looked up from the Gospel of Mark she was reading. Had someone stopped outside her cell door, or was it just her imagination? She had been alone in the cell for six weeks now with nothing to keep her company except a troop of ants and the silent daily visit of a trusty to deliver food and empty her toilet bucket. When a key clicked in the lock, she knew she hadn't been imagining. She quickly slipped the Gospel of Mark under the mattress. A moment later, a tall, thin guard stepped into the room. Corrie didn't recognize her as one of the usual guards.

"ten Boom, follow me," she ordered in a gruff voice.

Corrie climbed from the cot and reached for her coat.

119

"No, don't bother with that," said the guard. "Hurry up."

As Corrie scurried down the corridor after the guard, she wondered where they were taking her this time. It couldn't be back to the hospital in Scheveningen; she would need her hat and coat to leave the prison, and besides, she was feeling much better now.

The guard wound her way down several corridors, leading Corrie through areas of the prison she had never seen before. Every so often, Corrie heard a person talking or sobbing behind a cell door and wished she were able to stop and have a real conversation with another human being. But she kept on walking, and to her surprise, she was led outside after all. A blast of cold air wrapped itself around her as she stood in a small courtyard with four wooden huts crowded into it. All of the huts were painted gray and looked dull, like everything else in the prison, except for the hut on the far side of the courtyard. It was different. Around its dull, gray exterior was planted a row of yellow tulips. The tulips were past their prime, and the petals on many of the flowers were beginning to fall off, but that made no difference to Corrie. They were real flowers, and even if they were wilting, they were still the most beautiful things she had seen in a long time. Much to her delight, Corrie got to walk right past the tulips as the guard led her to the hut and motioned her to go in.

"Shut the door please, Miss ten Boom," a soft voice ordered from the far end of the hut.

Corrie did as she was told and then turned to see who it was that had spoken. It was a medium-build man with sandy brown hair and dressed in full Nazi uniform, complete with a row of ribbons and medals. Much to Corrie's surprise, the man was smiling at her.

"My name is Lieutenant Rahms," he said courteously, removing his hat. "Please sit down." He motioned for Corrie to sit in the armchair beside the woodstove.

"Thank you," mumbled Corrie, unused to being treated with kindness.

"You look a little cold, and I have read in your files that you have not been well. Before we begin our conversation, let me put a few more logs on the fire." The lieutenant reached into the woodpile.

Corrie felt the warm glow of the fire on her as he opened the door of the stove and pushed three pieces of wood into it. How wonderful it felt, and so did the armchair, which had a padded back and thick cushions. Corrie felt as though she were in a dream. Then suddenly she came to her senses. There was a reason the lieutenant was treating her this way. She had been warned about this before she ever got to prison. Some of the Nazi interrogators tried to get information out of members of the underground by torturing them, but other interrogators used kindness to lull their prisoners into thinking they had a friend in the Gestapo. There and then Corrie promised herself she would keep her guard up. Too many lives depended on her keeping quiet about the things she knew.

Lieutenant Rahms finished stoking the fire and sat down in a chair opposite Corrie. "Now, let me see," he said. "There are a few matters we need to clear up. I am going to ask you some questions, and I want you to answer as best you can."

Corrie nodded, amazed at the near perfect Dutch he spoke with only the slightest hint of a German accent.

The lieutenant reached into his breast pocket and casually pulled out a brown leather notebook. He flipped it open as he chatted. "Miss ten Boom," he began, "as you know, many mistakes are made during unfortunate times like these. I don't believe you should be in prison, and I want to help you find a way to get out of here. Would you like that?"

Corrie nodded. Who wouldn't like that?

"But," he continued in a soothing voice, "I can help you only if you tell me the whole truth. If you tell me everything you know, I'll see what I can do for you. How would that be?" he asked smiling.

Corrie smiled weakly back at him, trying to appear calmer than she really was.

"Good," replied the lieutenant. "Now, I am going to read you a list of names, and I want you to tell me which of them you recognize."

Corrie nodded.

"Joel Colijn?" he paused, looked at Corrie and then went on. "Hans Frederiks?" The list went on and on.

Corrie relaxed and sank back into the warm embrace of the armchair as she listened. She had nothing to hide from the lieutenant; she really didn't recognize a single name on the list. She supposed the names were all members of the underground, but everyone she knew in the underground was called Smit. Corrie had no idea of their real names. So there was absolutely nothing she could tell him about the names in his little book.

When the lieutenant had finished reading all the names, he looked at Corrie. "Are you sure you don't recognize even one of these names? It would be a great help to me, and it would help you, too," he said softly.

Corrie shook her head. "I don't know any of them," she said.

For the next hour Lieutenant Rahms asked her all sorts of questions about the underground. Corrie had the impression he thought she was deeply involved in the business of getting extra ration cards, either by organizing raids on food offices or by using forged papers. Of all the things the underground did, this was the one area Corrie knew the least about what went on. She had only distributed the extra ration cards other members of the underground had obtained. So again it was easy for her to say nothing about how the underground got their extra ration cards. There was little she could have told him even if she had wanted to.

Finally, Lieutenant Rahms stopped asking specific questions and looked Corrie in the eye. "I can see you are an honest woman," he said. "Why don't I sit here and you tell me about the things you were involved in before you came to this prison."

Corrie eagerly sat up straight in the armchair.

Now she had something to talk about. "Well, lieutenant," she began. "My family and I have always been involved in telling others about Jesus Christ. Only the week before I was arrested, I visited one of the girls I had worked with for many years. She is mentally retarded, but I am sure she understands that God loves her."

"What a stupid waste of time!" exclaimed the lieutenant. "Why would God love someone who is defective? What good is a religion that accepts half-wits into its midst? The Third Reich accepts only those among us who are worthy specimens."

Corrie smiled. "I would like to tell you the truth, if I may, lieutenant," she announced to him.

The officer leaned forward in his chair. "Of course, go right ahead," he said, picking up a pencil.

Corrie took a deep breath. She knew it was crazy to say what she was about to say to a Nazi officer, but it was the truth, and he had asked for it. "You and I are human, and we look on the outside of a person, but God looks at a person's heart. He knows whether there is light or darkness inside the person, and that is what is important to Him."

Lieutenant Rahms did not say anything, so Corrie went on. "Some people have great darkness in their hearts. Are you one of those people, lieutenant?"

"Today's session is over," he replied coldly as he got up from his chair and flung the door open. "Guard," he yelled, "take this prisoner back to her cell."

Corrie took one last look at the tulips as she was led from the lieutenant's office back to her cell.

For the rest of the day and well into the night, Corrie wondered whether she had done the right thing. She had made Lieutenant Rahms angry, and he was the only person who had offered to help her get out of prison. Had she gone too far in telling him the truth?

Surprisingly, the guard came for her the next morning and the following two mornings after that. Each time, Corrie was taken to the tulip-encircled hut, and each time, Lieutenant Rahms was waiting for her with an extra log to stoke the fire. However, he did not ask her any more questions about the underground. Instead, he asked lots of questions about God and the Bible. He told Corrie that his wife and children were in Bremen back in Germany, and every morning he hoped they had lived through another night. He also confided to her that some mornings he wished he hadn't awakened at all. He hated his job at the prison, and he hated being a Nazi, but he could see no way out.

At last, Corrie understood what Betsie had been trying to tell her from the time the first German bombs had fallen on Holland. Many of the Germans were just as much victims of Adolf Hitler and his horrible Third Reich as were the Dutch. They, too, lived in fear for their lives and the lives of their families.

After four visits, Lieutenant Rahms announced he had finished his investigation and sent Corrie back to her cell for the last time. She didn't expect to see him again, but she was wrong. About a week later, her cell door swung open, and the lieutenant himself was standing there. "Follow me," he said kindly.

Corrie tried to straighten her matted hair as she stood up. She stepped into the corridor and followed the lieutenant. "Where are we going?" she felt comfortable enough to ask him, her heart racing wildly.

"I am taking you back to my office, where there will be a reading," he replied.

"A reading?" Corrie repeated, thinking back to the wonderful evenings of play reading Leendert had organized for the guests at the Beje. But what could Lieutenant Rahms possibly mean by a reading?

"You told me your father died in this prison three months ago, did you not?" he asked matter-of-factly.

"Yes," answered Corrie.

"Well, the lawyer is here to read the will to the family. That is the legal way it is done in Holland."

Corrie was not sure she understood. Why was he, a Nazi officer, worried about the legal way things were done in Holland? It didn't make any sense—a German invader who cared about the laws of Holland? Maybe the lieutenant hadn't been acting all the time after all; maybe he really did care.

Then another wonderful thought struck Corrie. Would she be at the reading alone, or did the lieutenant mean that her family would be waiting in his office? She didn't dare ask him, but she felt a spring in her step as she followed him down the corridor. They rounded the last corner and stepped out into the familiar courtyard. Lieutenant Rahms opened the door into his office for Corrie.

"Nollie!" Corrie's eyes grew wide with joy. "And Willem, Betsie, Tine, Flip. It's really you, you're here," she said over and over again as she hugged and rehugged each of them.

Corrie turned to hear the door click shut. Lieutenant Rahms was gone. "He must be waiting outside, we're alone," she said, almost unable to believe her good fortune.

"Quickly, take these before he comes back," Nollie said, handing Corrie and Betsie each a small Bible.

They both slipped the precious cargo into their coat pockets and thanked Nollie.

"Now tell me everything," urged Corrie, turning around to make sure the door was still shut. "We might not have much time."

Sitting arm in arm, the ten Boom family exchanged their news.

Willem had managed to find out a little about their father's death. He had caught pneumonia within a couple of days of arriving at the prison. Finally, the other men in his cell had convinced the guards he needed medical help. But it was too late; he died lying on a stretcher alone outside the hospital. No one knew who he was, so as far as they had been able to determine, he had been buried in an unmarked grave. Corrie wept quietly as she listened.

Next Tine told them about Kik. He had been captured trying to smuggle a downed American airman to the North Sea coastline, where he was to be picked up and transported back to England. Tine and Willem had heard he'd been taken on a prison train into Germany.

"And what of the 'clocks' in the house?" Corrie wanted to know.

Flip told her the story. When everyone arrested at the Beje had been marched out of the police headquarters and onto the bus, Arnold had not been with them. Of course, he had been trapped by the raid and was one of those hiding in the Angels' Den. His father was sure he had been at the Beje at the time of the raid, so he started asking questions among his friends. Did anyone know of somewhere at the Beje where a man in the underground might hide? Amazingly, one of the people he asked was the man who had built the hidden room, and once he found out who Arnold's father was, he gladly told him about the hiding place in the third-floor bedroom. Next Arnold's father talked to a Haarlem policeman whom he trusted, and a plan was hatched. The following evening, the Gestapo were going to hand over the job of patrolling the Beje to the local police. On the night of Wednesday, March 1, two days after the raid, the Dutch policemen who took over from the Gestapo found the entrance to the Angels' Den and knocked on it. The wall slid open, and out came six people, four Jews, Mary, Martha, Eusie, and Ronnie, and the two members of the underground,

Hans and Arnold. Hans and Arnold thanked the policemen for rescuing them and slipped out onto the rooftop of the Beje. They jumped onto the roof of the house next door and disappeared into the night. The four Jewish "guests" waited quietly inside with the policemen until an underground worker came and guided them to safety. Then the policemen slid the door of the Angels' Den closed and went back to standing guard outside the Beje. As far as Flip knew, the Gestapo still hadn't found the Angels' Den.

Corrie could hardly believe what she was hearing. She had been so worried about the guests. Silently she thanked God; there were still good men in Holland like the policemen who had risked their lives for the guests at the Beje.

Just as Flip finished telling the story, the door opened and Lieutenant Rahms stepped inside. "Has the will been read yet?" he asked politely.

The Dutch lawyer who had been standing in the corner of the room indicated it had not and then opened a large envelope, pulled out a document, and began to read. There were no surprises in the will. Casper ten Boom's only belonging of any value was the Beje and its clockshop, which he left to Betsie and Corrie as long as they chose to live there.

When the reading was finished, the lieutenant walked over to Corrie. "You must go now," he ordered.

Corrie took one long, last look at her brother and sisters and stumbled out the door. She could hear Betsie being escorted out behind her.

When she got back to her cell she felt lonelier than ever. She lay on her cot and relived every moment of the visit. She was worried about Willem and Betsie. Although Willem was out of prison, he looked thin and weak, and Betsie, with her blood disease, was paler than Corrie could ever remember seeing her. Corrie also thought about her father's will. The words the lawyer had read echoed in her mind: "Elizabeth and Cornelia can have the Beje as long as they choose to live there." After all the family had been through there, Corrie couldn't imagine living anywhere else but in that wonderful house on Barteljorisstraat in Haarlem. But before she could live there again, she had to survive her present nightmare.

Chapter 11

The Word Struck Terror

All prisoners, collect your things together and stand by your door," barked the voice of the guard. Corrie stood up; she had been crouching, having a "conversation" with a visiting ant. It was just after breakfast on June 12, 1944, and she had been a prisoner now for three and a half months.

Corrie scooped up the Bible Nollie had given her, placed it in her coat pocket, and stood by the door, her heart thumping wildly. What could it be? The other times she had left her cell it had been alone, but this time the guard was yelling for the whole prison block to prepare to move. Had the Allied Forces landed in Holland? Were they about to be freed? She stood eagerly by the door and waited for it to be unlocked. But nothing happened.

131

Lunchtime came and went, and still the door stayed locked. No one brought the usual slice of bread for lunch, and Corrie's stomach began to churn. Was it just a mean trick the guards were playing on them, trying to make everyone think they were leaving while they sat in their common room laughing at the stupid prisoners? Corrie was beginning to wonder.

Finally, at midafternoon, the door was unlocked and swung open. "Hurry up," a guard Corrie had never seen before yelled into her cell. "Fall into a line and march. Now!"

Corrie stepped out into the corridor, eager to see other human beings. The whole place was crowded with dirty, thin women. Even though Corrie didn't recognize any of them, she wanted to hug each one. They were fellow prisoners, and they were all living the same nightmare she was.

Like streams joining a river, the women in the cells near Corrie's joined the throng of prisoners marching along the corridor. As they marched, one word was whispered up and down the line of prisoners. "Invasion." Corrie hoped it was true. Maybe she would be free soon.

Before long, about one thousand men and women prisoners were standing in the courtyard. Corrie craned her neck looking for an auburn bun belonging to Betsie. Before she could spot her sister, Corrie was herded onto a large bus. The windows had been painted over and all the seats removed. "Move up, move up," yelled a guard, with his hand on his rifle to help get his point across. Corrie felt herself being squeezed from all sides. "More, more," yelled the guard. "Do you think this is a sightseeing trip?" He laughed loudly at his own joke as he shoved the women closer together and waved for more to get on the bus.

When the guard was finally satisfied that not another body could be packed in, the bus lurched off. It swung dangerously around corners, and there was nothing to hold on to, but no one fell; everyone was packed in too tightly.

About twenty minutes later, the bus stopped and the door opened. Corrie was carried along from the bus by the crowd.

"Fall back into lines!" another guard yelled outside the bus, and Corrie shuffled into position, daring to turn her head slightly as she did so. The prisoners were on a large paved area beside a railroad track. There were no trains in sight, and the sun was beginning to set. Corrie had had nothing to eat since the meager breakfast prisoners were fed, and she felt weak and hungry. She hoped they would get some food to eat soon.

"Stand still," bellowed a guard as he slammed his rifle butt with all his might into the stomach of a woman. Corrie shut her eyes and prayed as the woman doubled over and collapsed. It was so hard to watch such needless cruelty.

For more than an hour, bus after bus brought more human cargo. Like most of the other prisoners, Corrie studied each new group that arrived.

She desperately wanted to catch a glimpse of Betsie. And then finally she saw an auburn bun. It had to be Betsie! As the woman in front of her shifted from one leg to the other, Corrie caught a better view. Her heart leapt. It was Betsie. Corrie tried to keep an eye on Betsie as her head bobbed in and out of lines of people. Eventually, Betsie joined a line of prisoners about one hundred yards from where Corrie was standing. Corrie promised herself she would find a way to get to Betsie before the day was over.

Corrie stood and waited, feeling the bodies of the other women near her. After three and a half months on her own in a cell, it was wonderful to have other women so close. And when the guard was not patrolling nearby, Corrie looked up at the sky. Pink, puffy clouds slid across the horizon in front of the setting sun. Corrie thought it was the most beautiful thing she'd ever seen. Finally, as the last rays of sunlight streaked through the clouds, she heard a noise. It got louder and louder until Corrie knew for sure it was a train. It hissed to a stop in front of the prisoners, spewing billows of smoke and steam in their faces.

"Get on. Stay in your lines," ordered the guard as he opened the first carriage. Quickly the orderly line broke down, and the women, each one eager to claim a seat rather than be left standing, surged forward. Corrie saw her chance. She had to resist the crowd and elbow her way to Betsie. She gritted her teeth and slipped into a space between two women.

Like a swimmer fighting a strong current, Corrie struggled to avoid being swept into the train by the flow of the prisoners. Just when Corrie didn't think she had enough strength to do it, Betsie bobbed back into view. She was only three or four people in front of her now. With a dive, Corrie parted the crowd and grabbed her sister's hand. Betsie turned to see who it was. "Corrie! Thank God it's you, Corrie," she beamed as they were carried along and up into the train by the rest of the crowd. They were grateful that they were able to find a seat together.

For several minutes all the two sisters could do was to put their heads on each other's shoulder and weep. It was such a relief to be together again. As they sat and wept and talked, time sped by. Occasionally, Corrie looked out the window into the darkness and wondered where they were heading. But it did not seem to matter so much now that she had her big sister with her.

Eventually the train came to a stop. Everyone now peered out the window, trying to work out where they were.

"It looks like we are in the woods."

"I don't see a railway station."

"We were definitely going south; I saw the Delft Cathedral tower."

The comments flew throughout the train as everyone waited nervously to see what the Nazis had in store for them next.

"Hurry. Hurry. Get out of the train," a guard began yelling.

Corrie helped Betsie to her feet, and once again they joined the sorry flow of women prisoners, not knowing where they were going.

Once outside the train, they realized that they were indeed in the middle of a forest. Corrie breathed in the heady scent of pine that filled the air. It smelled better to her than expensive perfume. Again the prisoners were ordered to form rows. Then they were told to march. After walking for more than a mile, they emerged from the forest into a clearing.

"Vught," the woman to Corrie's right muttered. The word struck terror in Corrie, who had heard about this place from the prisoners in her first cell at Scheveningen. Vught was located in the south of Holland near Brabant, but it was not a Dutch prison. It was a German concentration camp especially designed for prisoners the Nazis thought were the most dangerous to them. Corrie could feel the dread rising inside her as they marched through the barbed-wire gates of the camp and into the first building. They were in a dining room with rows of long wooden tables. Corrie and Betsie found seats together, laid their heads side by side on a tabletop, and drifted off to sleep, exhausted from the trip.

Despite the fact that she was in a notorious concentration camp, Corrie was happier at Vught than she had been at Scheveningen. There were other people around to talk to, she slept next to her sister, and together they held Bible studies in the evenings for the other women prisoners. Everyone was given a job to do, and even though they worked for twelve hours every day, it was far better to Corrie than sitting alone in a cell with only ants for company. Corrie's job was at the "Phillip's Factory," one of the clapboard prison barracks buildings where prisoners put together radios for German fighter planes. Corrie started out sorting glass rods into groups by size, but when Mr. Moorman, a kind trusty who was her supervisor, found out she was a watchmaker, he gave her a much more technical job to do. At lunchtime, the workers were given half an hour off, and Corrie would use it to lie on the grass soaking up the sun.

But Corrie was worried about her sister. Betsie seemed to be getting weaker by the day. She was assigned to work in the sewing room, along with many of the other older prisoners and young mothers with babies. She told Corrie the work was easy, mainly mending uniforms and pillowcases. But after a few days, Corrie began to wonder. Betsie's hands were swollen, and one day she came back to the barracks with them wrapped in rags. After a lot of questioning, she admitted to Corrie that most of her day was spent braiding heavy ropes together. She hadn't told Corrie about it because she did not want her to worry. There were enough other things to worry about in Vught. But Corrie did worry. She wondered how long Betsie's weakened body would hold up under such difficult circumstances.

Back in Scheveningen, Corrie's world had been no bigger than her cell, but at Vught, she was surrounded by other people and their problems and difficulties. The woman who worked next to her putting together the radios had a baby one night, but the child was as weak as her mother and was dead by morning. A young Jewish girl received a letter telling her that her brother had been shot trying to steal some food. Now she was the only living member of her family left. The list went on and on. Every woman had a tale of misery to tell. Many of the women had husbands or sons locked up in the men's side of the concentration camp.

Spring turned into summer, and things began to get more tense in Vught. The guards exploded in rage at the littlest thing, and all the prisoners were punished for one person's "crime." More often, Corrie found herself lined up for roll call at four in the morning instead of the usual five o'clock. The women would have to stand at attention for the extra hour. Corrie continued to worry about Betsie, who was skinnier than ever, now weighing under ninety pounds. And Corrie's stomach particularly churned itself into knots with worry during the long roll calls. Corrie knew that the women who collapsed at roll call were punished with a trip to the bunkers, tiny cupboards the size of a coffin. The prisoner was locked inside one of the cupboards for the day with no air and no food. Many women never came back to the barracks after going to the bunkers. Corrie hoped and prayed Betsie wouldn't be one of them.

The concentration camp began to get over-crowded as prisoners from other prisons in Holland were brought there. Everyone waited for night to fall so that they could question the new arrivals. Mostly they had rumors to report, but sometimes someone had real information. By late July, there was talk of the Russian army invading Poland. And then in August, news began filtering into the camp of an invasion of France at Normandy by Allied Forces. According to rumor, the Allies had already liberated Paris. The prisoners hoped and prayed that it was true. In fact, it was. On June 6, 1944, the Allied Forces had begun the massive D-Day invasion of France. They had met fierce German opposition, but eventually they had prevailed and were now beginning to push the Germans back.

Rumor also had it that some of the Dutch troops who had escaped to England at the beginning of the occupation were on the move. The Princess Irene Brigade, as they called themselves, was pressing into Belgium and would march into southern Holland soon. Corrie thought that much of this news was probably true, and it would explain why the guards had become extra nasty. And then came news that Adolf Hitler had been injured by a bomb. Some of his own officers had apparently tried to kill him. Things were not going well for the Germans.

In late August came the first sign that an Allied invasion had indeed taken place. One day as Corrie lay in the noonday sun, she heard an airplane overhead, then a second and a third. Soon the sky was filled with steel gray aircraft, and not with the dreaded swastika emblem on their wings but with the red, white, and blue circles of the British air force. The other women sitting on the grass all sprang to their feet. No one stopped them as they waved and cheered at the bombers above until they were hoarse.

As the women watched, the sky suddenly erupted in flashes of orange. Antiaircraft guns were firing at the planes, and then German fighters swooped in from the northeast with their guns blazing. A huge air battle began. Planes were hit and billowed black smoke as they plummeted to the ground. Bits of shrapnel from the battle started to rain down on them. Some large pieces pelted the barracks, and five women were dragged off to the hospital wounded. Even so, there was a wonderful excitement in the concentration camp. Surely they would be rescued any day soon.

Corrie and Betsie began planning what they would do once they were freed. The Beje had been shut up for five months now. The rugs would need to be taken out onto the roof and beaten. Then there were the holes in the walls and floors where the Nazis had searched for the Angels' Den. They would have to get a good carpenter to fix it all up. And when it was all repaired, they would hold a big party to celebrate their return. All of their friends would be there.

A week later, though, Corrie was still twisting wires together for radios. As she did so, the whole building shook and was filled with a deafening boom. The massive explosion was not far away. Corrie felt her ears block up. "Swallow and then breathe with your mouth open," yelled Mr. Moorman as the workers all dived under the tables. Boom! Another explosion, and then another. The explosions continued for half an hour and then stopped as suddenly they had begun. One by one the prisoners crawled from their hiding places to discuss what it could all mean.

"The Allies must be bombing Brabant."

"Are you sure it wasn't cannons firing close by?"

"The Princess Irene Brigade is here; we'll be free by tomorrow."

Suggestions of what was happening buzzed around the room, and then Mr. Moorman spoke. "I don't think it was guns or cannons; it sounded like bombs. But I didn't hear them whistle like they do when they are falling from an airplane. And they were regular. My guess is that the Germans are blowing up bridges and buildings before they retreat. That's the way they've done it before."

Corrie believed Mr. Moorman, an intelligent man who had been the principal of a large Catholic school before the war. Mr. Moorman seemed to be right about most things. Corrie wondered what it would mean for the prisoners in Vught. Would they be set free? Corrie hoped more than anything that that's what would happen, but inside her she couldn't imagine anyone as cruel as their guards just opening the gates and letting them all go before they retreated. And she was right.

About an hour later, an announcement blared

over the camp loudspeakers. "Roll call for every-one. Return to your barracks immediately."

Nothing like this had ever happened before. Life followed a very strict routine in Vught concentra-tion camp. People were afraid. Men and women hugged each other desperately before the guards came in to hurry the prisoners along with their rifle butts.

Corrie rushed back to the barracks. A wave of relief swept over her when she found Betsie already there. The women lined up in front of the building and waited to see what would happen next. They didn't have to wait long. The air filled with pop-ping noises. Then silence and then another round of popping noises. "Guns! They're executing the men!" screamed one of the women as she collapsed. Other women began to sob and wail. Some yelled abuse and shrieked loudly at their German captors. The guards just turned and walked away.

For two hours the women stood together listen-ing to the horrible sound. And then, since no guards had returned, they drifted back into their barracks. Many of the women who had listened to the ten Boom sisters' Bible studies came to pray with Corrie and Betsie.

When they finally lay down to sleep that night, Betsie whispered to Corrie, "I am so grateful." Corrie looked at her sister and wondered what she could possibly be grateful about on such an awful day. Betsie put her arm around Corrie and continued. "I am so grateful our dear father died when he did. I couldn't bear to think of him living through any of this." Corrie felt a lump rising in her throat. Tears streamed down her cheeks. She cried for herself. She cried for Betsie. And she cried for every woman in the barracks.

All night long the room was filled with the sobbing and moaning of grieving women. Corrie could not sleep. She lay on her back wondering what it all meant for the women prisoners. Mr. Moorman must have been right; the Nazis were getting ready to retreat. Why else would they kill so many hard-working men? And then she tried to block the next thought from her mind, but it kept creeping back. If the Germans had killed the men prisoners today, were they planning to kill the women prisoners tomorrow?

Chapter 12

Number 66730

Gather your things together; you're moving out, now," screamed one of the female guards. Corrie looked at Betsie and breathed a sigh of relief. If they were taking their belongings with them, then probably they really were going to be transferred somewhere and not just lined up outside and shot like the men had been. So the two sisters stuffed their meager belongings into a pillowcase. There was a small bottle of vitamin drops from a Red Cross parcel; it was nearly empty, but they were trying to stretch it as far as possible. Nollie had sent Betsie a blue woolen sweater. Amazingly, the package containing it had reached her in Vught. Corrie stuffed the sweater into the pillowcase. Their belongings barely made a bump in the bottom of the pillowcase as Corrie swung it over her shoulder. The only other thing they owned was too precious to put in the pillowcase. It was the small Bible Nollie had given Corrie at the reading of their father's will. Betsie had made a small cloth pouch for it in the sewing room, and it always hung around one of their necks. Nollie had given Betsie a Bible at the same time, but Betsie had given it to another needy woman. So now she and Corrie shared Corrie's Bible. Their belongings in hand, the two sisters lined up for one last roll call at Vught concentration camp.

After roll call the women were marched five abreast out of the camp. A large truck was parked at the gate. As each line of prisoners marched past the truck, it was stopped for a moment, and every woman in the line was handed a blanket. This made no sense to Corrie. They had just left blankets in their barracks, so why take the time to hand out new ones? Corrie couldn't think of an answer, but then, so many things the Germans did made no sense to her. Since the blankets were thick, much too heavy for Betsie to carry in her weakened state, Corrie carried Betsie's blanket as well as her own as they marched away from the camp.

The women retraced the route they had marched to Vught from the train. When they reached the railroad tracks, a guard ordered them to halt. Corrie peered up and down the track but saw no passenger train like the one that had brought them from Scheveningen, only a line of large boxcars. German soldiers were perched on top of them, their machine guns pointed at the women. Once Corrie would have been terrified if someone pointed a gun at her. Now she thought nothing of it.

The woman to the left of Corrie looked up at the soldiers. "What does it matter if they shoot us now, we are all going to die anyway," she said.

Corrie reached out her hand to comfort the woman. She wanted to say, "That's not true, don't think like that," but it would be a lie. After all, look at what the Nazis had done to the men the day before.

A tall, dark-haired soldier marched the length of the train unlocking the boxcars and sliding their doors open. Corrie gasped. She knew what was going to happen. All the women, about one thousand of them, were going to be pushed into the boxcars, which had no windows or seats and weren't designed to carry animals, much less human beings!

"Move it, you old cows, we've got to get eighty of you in each car," a guard near Corrie yelled. Corrie felt a gun press into her back, and together the women surged onto the boxcar. Several of them had to help Betsie up, as it was too high for her to climb. Once inside, they moved as far back as they could as more women were ordered into the boxcar. Finally, when Corrie could hardly breathe, the door was slid shut. The women were alone in total darkness.

At first they all panicked. Women screamed and clawed at the walls, but after about an hour, they calmed down enough to organize themselves. They found that if each woman sat with her legs apart like on a bobsled, there was enough room for them all to sit on the floor of the boxcar. They tucked their blankets around themselves and waited. During the rest of the day the boxcar was shunted backwards and forwards, never moving more than a few feet in either direction as the boxcars were connected to form a long train. Inside, women needed to go to the bathroom, but there was no bucket—and no way to climb over the wall of bodies to get to one even if there had been. They had no choice but to go right where they were sitting. Corrie didn't know which was worse, the embarrassment or the stench. By nightfall, some of the women sitting near the sides of the boxcar had managed to gouge some small holes in the timber, and some fresh air trickled in. About the same time, the women heard popping noises against the outside of the boxcar. They all sat still and listened.

"Sounds like hailstones," whispered one of the women.

"No, it's not on the roof; it's just hitting the side of the car," said another woman.

"Machine guns," said yet another woman.

They were being fired upon! This could mean only one thing. The Allied Forces must be very close. Excitement filled the boxcar. At any moment the doors could be flung open and they could be free. But neither happened. Half an hour later, they felt the train begin to move, slowly at first, then gathering speed. The excitement left the boxcar as quickly as it had come. The women sat in silence. There was no need to say anything; it was obvious they were headed east into Germany. Where else was there left to take them?

"Why are they bothering to take us to Germany? We are a group of weak, half-starved Dutch women. Why would they waste a train trip on us?" Corrie asked out loud. No one in the boxcar could think of an answer.

The train sped on. The boxcar smelled so disgusting that Corrie had to force herself to breathe. The women near the holes in the side of the boxcar yelled out to notify the others when it got dark or light. First one night passed, then another, and then a third. Finally, the train ground to a halt. The women heard the sound of young boys yelling in German, and then the door to the boxcar slid open. Corrie raised her arm to shield her eyes from the intense light that spilled in.

The pressure of eighty women packed into such a tiny space pushed out those near the door. The women fell the four feet onto the stones beside the railroad track. More of the women inside the boxcar crawled towards the fresh air. They were all too exhausted to do anything more than fall out of the doorway on top of the others. Soon there were large piles of women outside the doors of every boxcar in the train. Slowly, the stronger women pulled themselves free of the piles. There was a small lake about twenty feet from the train, and the women began to crawl towards it. Corrie was one of them. She left Betsie in the pile of women and promised to come back for her. Over the rough rocks she crawled, her knees bleeding as she went, her eyes fixed firmly on the water in front of her.

Finally, Corrie collapsed beside the lake. She sank her face into the water. How wonderful it felt! She let it lap over her hair and around her neck. She gulped mouthfuls of it. All along the lake edge, other women were doing the same.

After a few minutes, Corrie felt strong enough to sit up. She looked around. Unlike the guards in Holland who were grown men and women, the guards here were teenage boys. Some of them didn't even look fifteen years old. Corrie shook her head. Over a thousand women were being controlled by seven teenage boys with guns. In truth, there was no need for more than seven guards; none of the women had the strength to resist.

One of the young guards carrying a pile of canvas bags threw one down near Corrie. "Carry water," he barked in German.

Corrie dipped the bag into the lake and stood up. Her whole body wobbled as she staggered back to the train with the water. Betsie had managed to crawl a little distance from the pile of other women. Corrie found her and poured some water over her. "Thank you," she mouthed through her cracked lips. Corrie went on, pouring water into other prisoners' mouths. Some of them, though, were unconscious, and the eyes of others were rolled back in their sockets. Corrie knew they were dead.

When the water was gone, Corrie handed the canvas bag to another prisoner and lay down beside Betsie. It was a beautiful, sunny day. Birds cheeped in nearby trees, and a German farmer drove his horse and hay cart down the road beside the railroad track. It all seemed so normal, except for the dead and dying women lying beside the train.

"Get up. Get moving," screamed one of the young guards, hitching up his uniform pants, which were too big for him. Corrie stayed where she was. *How easy it would be to give up right now,* she thought. *Betsie and I could die together, lying in the sun, listening to the birds.*

"Come on, we have to get up." Betsie's voice broke into her thoughts. Corrie turned her head to look at her sister. She could clearly see the bones beneath her skin and the shape of her skull beneath her thin, gaunt face. Betsie's lips were dry and cracked. Corrie scrambled to her feet. If her big sister could go on, so could she.

Supporting each other, Corrie and Betsie joined the ragtag line of women that had begun disappearing over a small rise to the right of the train past the small lake. Slowly, the two sisters climbed to the top of the rise. By the time they got there, Betsie was completely out of breath. They stood for a moment looking down from the rise. The sight laid out below made Corrie close her eyes in fear and dread. Stretching as far as she could see was row upon row of gray clapboard buildings, just like the ones they had left in Vught. A huge brick wall with barbed wire along its top surrounded the buildings, and towards the front of the compound was a large concrete building with a huge smokestack protruding from its center. Blue-gray smoke belched from it.

Even as Corrie stood with her eyes closed, the reality of where they were could not be shut out. "God help us, it's Ravensbruck," whispered one of the other women. Corrie reached out to steady herself against her sister. She had heard of Ravensbruck; everyone in Holland had. It was a death camp for women. A place that thousands of women were forced into by the Nazis but from which few ever came out alive.

Betsie whispered into Corrie's ear, "Remember, there is no pit so deep that God's love is not deeper."

Corrie nodded.

Still clutching their pillowcase, Corrie and Betsie marched down the hill and into the notorious Ravensbruck concentration camp with the hundreds of other women from Vught who were still alive after their journey from Holland. To the left of the main gate was a large open area covered with straw, and the women were herded into it and told to wait. Corrie sighed. There it was again; the Germans were always getting them to hurry up just so they could wait at the other end. As the women reached the straw, they sank down onto it. Corrie and Betsie found a spot, too.

"Oh, no!" exclaimed a prisoner near them as she leapt to her feet. "Lice, the place is alive with lice."

And so it was. Corrie looked at the straw that was seething with tiny, biting insects. The women looked at each other as if to say, what can we do? They were too weak to stand any longer. They had no choice but to flop down on the louse-infested straw. After an hour or so, all the women were again seated on the straw. And then the haircutting began. The Nazis did not order it; the women did it themselves. Several women had scissors, which were slowly passed from woman to woman. They began to cut off each other's hair. When the scissors were handed to her, with tears in her eyes, Corrie cut off Betsie's once beautiful auburn hair. Next Betsie cut off Corrie's hair. As it fell to the ground, Corrie noticed that in the short time she had been a prisoner of the Nazis, her hair had turned from dark brown to gray.

The women sat on the straw for the rest of the day and on through the night. It rained heavily, and their blankets were soaked. Betsie started to cough; at first she coughed up phlegm, later blood. Corrie helped her put on Nollie's woolen sweater, but it did not help much. Throughout the night and all the next day, Corrie had to help Betsie to the ditch the women were using as a toilet. For two full days they were left sitting on the louse-infested straw with only a slice of black bread and cup of so-called coffee twice a day to keep them alive.

Finally, as night was about to fall on the third day, a guard yelled for the women to line up and follow him. They filed past a desk, where each woman was given a number. Corrie was prisoner number 66730, and Betsie was number 66729.

Next, the women were counted off into groups of fifty and told to wait. Since Corrie was at the front of her group, she could see what was happening. The first group of fifty women were told to leave all their belongings, including the blankets, in a pile by the door of a long, low building. No one was recording who had left what behind. Corrie's heart chilled. That could mean only one thing; they were not going to get the things back. After the women had handed over their belongings, they were told to strip naked and step into the building. For fifteen horrible minutes Corrie thought they had been ushered into a gas chamber. Then, to her relief, she caught sight of the women coming out of a door at the far end of the building. They were all wearing thin cotton dresses with a large "X" sewn on the front and on the back.

Panic gripped Corrie as she watched. What would she and Betsie do without their Bible? And Betsie needed the warm woolen sweater Nollie had sent her, too. "God," she prayed as she stood waiting for their turn to be processed, "please help me to find a way to get these things through."

Just then, Betsie doubled over. "My stomach," she groaned. "I have to get to a bathroom fast."

Corrie looked around. They were too far away from the ditch they had used for the past few days. Bravely she stepped out of line and spoke to a guard. "My sister has to go to the bathroom now. She is sick; she cannot wait."

The guard looked at the two of them and

growled, "Over there. Use the shower drain." He pointed his rifle towards the entrance the naked women had gone in.

Corrie helped Betsie to the showers, which were in a huge, dark, damp room with a row of moldy chairs stacked at the far end. In a flash, Corrie had an inspiration. "Quick, Betsie, take off your sweater," she said.

Without questioning, Betsie took it off and handed it to her sister.

"Watch for the guards," Corrie whispered as she pulled the Bible and its pouch over her head. She ran the length of the shower building and tucked the Bible, bottle of vitamin drops, and blue woolen sweater between the chairs. In less than a minute she was back beside Betsie.

"Let's get back into line, quickly," she said, helping Betsie up.

Once in line again they had another half hour to wait until it was their turn to strip and shower. The whole dehumanizing process was made bearable by the fact that they had their things waiting for them near the exit to the showers.

A pile of well-worn dresses was dumped on the floor, and the women scrambled to find one that fit them. Corrie found the perfect dress for Betsie. It had long sleeves, which would hide the sweater underneath. Betsie put it on while Corrie found a dress for herself. In the confusion of the other women trying to find a dress that fit, Corrie slipped away and recovered the things she had hidden between the chairs. She pulled the pouch with the Bible in it over her head. She slipped the bottle of vitamin drops inside the pouch as well, and she tied the sweater around her waist under her dress. Then she rejoined the group.

"Line up by the door," yelled a guard who had just walked in.

Corrie's heart sank as she joined the line. Three more guards had appeared, and by hand they were searching each woman from head to toe. They would surely feel the sweater and the pouch in an instant. "God," she prayed again in desperation, "we can go through anything if we have this Bible with us. Please send your angels to hide it from the guards."

Corrie took a deep breath; the woman in front of her was being searched. It would be her turn next. But her turn never came. Instead the guard reached right past her and began to search Betsie. Corrie just kept walking. Later, when she talked to the other women processed that day, Corrie discovered she was the only one who had not been searched. Tears ran down her cheeks as she thanked God for protecting the Bible, and she wondered about what lay ahead for the ten Boom sisters.

Chapter 13

Passed Inspection

Many thousands of prisoners were being held in Ravensbruck concentration camp. Corrie and Betsie and the other women from Vught soon fell into the dull routine of life there. Every morning they were awakened by a whistle at four o'clock. A slice of black bread and cup of hot "coffee" were provided for breakfast, and then all prisoners were to be lined up in rows of ten outside their barracks by four-thirty. Sometimes they stood in line until six or seven in the morning. At first this was not so bad, but as fall turned into early winter, many of the women could not stand in the cold for that long. A thud would be heard as someone hit the ground, followed by the footsteps and shouts of guards. Every prisoner knew what would happen next, but it was seldom talked about in the camp—it was too awful.

Ravensbruck had a large gas chamber where weak and disobedient prisoners were put to death. Often, rumor had it, a prisoner was tricked into thinking she was going to have a shower before being sent to the hospital. She would strip of her clothes willingly, accept a fresh bar of soap, and join other prisoners "showering" in the room. Soon the metal doors would slam shut, and within minutes the surprised and terrified prisoners would be dead from breathing the poisonous gas that was let into the chamber. The bodies would then be thrown into a large incinerator that burned night and day.

After roll call, the women would go to their work assignments. At first, Corrie and Betsie worked side by side at the nearby Siemens factory. Siemens was a large German industrial company that supplied Hitler's army. At the factory, the two sisters, along with hundreds of other sick and dying women, were made to push huge boxcars filled with scrap iron along the railroad track and inside the building, where they unloaded the boxcars by hand into huge bins. Sometimes a piece of iron would weigh hundreds of pounds, and a group of women would work together to heave it into a bin.

The women worked beside German workers who were paid wages for their labor and came to work with cheese sandwiches and boiled eggs for lunch and at night went home to wives and children. Although they worked within a few feet of each other, the German workers never once looked over at the women from Ravensbruck.

After twelve hours of backbreaking work, the women were marched back to the concentration camp, where they were given watery soup for dinner and then locked in their barracks for the night.

Corrie and Betsie were in Barracks 28, a long, low room. Instead of having cots to sleep on, it had rows of wide shelves stacked three high. Each shelf was only about two feet above the one below. The women were expected to sleep on the shelves. On her first night in the barracks, Corrie had been overcome by the noise and the horrible stench of vomit and human waste. The next morning, she found out why. One of the prisoners told her there were over fourteen hundred women packed into a barracks designed to hold only four hundred. And those fourteen hundred women were locked in at night, with only eight backed-up toilets to use. Corrie decided that if ever there was hell on earth, Ravensbruck must be it. She had never imagined a more dirty, overcrowded, and cruel place could exist than Vught.

On top of that, Barracks 28 had the reputation of being the most flea-infested barracks in all Ravensbruck. Because of this, the guards would stand at the door and bark orders, but they virtually never set foot inside. At first Corrie had hated the fleas, but when she found they kept the guards away, she was grateful for them. At night, the ten Boom sisters could hold Bible studies and prayer meetings for the other prisoners without being caught.

At first just a handful of women were interested in listening to the Bible study, but slowly the mood in the barracks changed, and many women wanted to hear what the sisters had to say. Of course, in Ravensbruck not all the women were Dutch. Women from all over Europe were imprisoned there, and a system for reading the Bible so they could all understand was soon developed. Betsie would read the Bible passage in Dutch and German, and then other women in the room would translate it into French, Italian, Polish, and Russian. Night after night the women listened to the Bible being read in this way. And after Betsie had shared about God's love for them all, they would sing a hymn together and pray. Soon Barracks 28 became known as the "crazy barracks where the women have hope."

As winter approached, the women who went to work in the Seimens factory were each issued a coat. Then one morning they were not sent to the factory at all. Instead, Corrie and Betsie found themselves sitting on their "bed" in the barracks knitting gray socks for soldiers. No one knew for sure why they no longer went to the factory. Some women were sure it had been hit by Allied bombs. After all, nearby Berlin was now a constant target of bombs from Allied aircraft.

Betsie was a lightning-fast knitter and finished her quota of socks for the day long before anyone else. As soon as she had knitted the last stitch, she would take the Bible from its pouch and begin reading it aloud. Groups of women knitted quietly and listened as she shared about the importance of what she had read. Betsie encouraged the women to pray for the men who would be wearing the socks they were knitting. At first they laughed at her. It was impossible to think of praying for German soldiers. Surely God didn't expect them to do that? But Betsie read them passages about how Jesus had forgiven the men who nailed Him to the cross. And they recited the Lord's Prayer together: "Forgive us our trespasses as we forgive those who trespass against us." And slowly many of the women began to see and understand what being a Christian was really all about.

Even though knitting was easier than factory work, Corrie began to worry more about Betsie's health. Betsie coughed and coughed during the long morning roll calls, and when Corrie took her to the hospital, she was told that Betsie was not sick enough to be examined by a doctor. No one with a temperature under 104 degrees was seen by a doctor!

There was nothing Corrie could do for her sister but watch and pray. She noticed that when Betsie was holding a Bible study, she seemed quite normal, but the rest of the time, she seemed to be in a sort of dream. She would lie in her sleeping space and say to Corrie, "We will be free before the new year. I can see us walking the streets of Haarlem together. Yes, by New Year's Day 1945, we will be free."

Corrie would hug her tightly with tears streaming down her face. Then Betsie would go on, "Corrie, think of all the people who will need our help when the war ends. We will find a place for them to come to. It will be a beautiful place. There will be huge gardens, and the floors will be made of inlaid wood." Then she would speak as though she were standing in the entrance hall of such a place. "Look," she would say, "there are marble statues set in little nooks all along the walls. And the staircase, it is so wide, and the windows are tall, right to the roof."

Corrie often wondered whether her sister was imagining heaven when she spoke like that.

With all her might, Corrie hoped and prayed that the war would be over soon so that Betsie could get the medical help she so desperately needed. Every day, Betsie had less energy than the day before. Finally, one morning in mid-December, it happened. Betsie collapsed during roll call. The guards came for her and dragged her away. But she was taken not to the gas chamber but to the camp hospital. Later that day, after she had finished her knitting, Corrie sneaked into the hospital to see Betsie. Betsie was lying comfortably in a bed. Corrie smiled at her. What a luxury—she had a whole cot to herself! But as ill as Betsie obviously was, she told Corrie she still had not been examined by a doctor. As Corrie bent over the bed to kiss her sister good-bye, Betsie grabbed her arm. Her eyes were shining brightly. "We must tell them, Corrie. We must tell them there is no pit so deep that God's love cannot reach it."

The next morning after roll call, Corrie raced back to see Betsie. She decided to check through the window first to see whether the way was clear. Corrie rubbed a clear patch in the icy glass and peered in. There were two nurses next to Betsie's bed. One was standing at the head of the bed and the other at the foot. As Corrie stared, they each lifted the corners of the bedsheet and carried it down the corridor with Betsie on it. Corrie stood rooted to the spot by the window. Her eyes had seen it, but her mind refused to accept it. Her big sister, her best friend, was dead. The nurses were carrying her body to the incinerator.

Finally, Corrie backed away from the window and walked to the barracks. When she got there, the other women clamored for news of Betsie. A sad hush fell over the room as Corrie told them what she had seen.

Even though she was surrounded by so many women, the next two days were the loneliest of Corrie's life, lonelier than when she had been locked up by herself in Scheveningen. She felt numb. Tears streamed across her cheeks, and she was lost in her thoughts. Instead of their being free before the new year, Betsie was dead. How could it be? And as if her grief at losing Betsie weren't enough, a terrible rumor that all women over fifty were soon to be "exterminated" made its way around the barracks. According to the rumor, Ravensbruck was running out of food to feed all the prisoners, so it had been decided to reduce the number of prisoners in the camp by gassing the older ones. When Corrie heard this, despite her grief, she was glad Betsie had gone to be in a better place.

On December 17, 1944, three days after Betsie's death, the morning roll call went as usual, that is, until dismissal. The whistle blew, and then, "ten Boom, Cornelia, remain behind," bellowed through the loudspeaker. Corrie started to march away with the others. Even though she had heard the announcement, she had been number 66730 for so long that she hardly recognized her own name. Slowly the words sank in, and she stopped marching. They had called her by name. Names were never used in Ravensbruck. She tried to think what it could mean. What could the Nazis want with her now? Had someone reported her for visiting Betsie in the hospital? Or for holding Bible studies in the barracks? Corrie didn't know. But whatever it was, she hoped she would be able to sit down soon. In the past few weeks her legs had become so swollen and the skin was stretched so tight across them that it stung when she stood.

"Follow me," barked a guard. Corrie did her best to keep up. She followed the guard all the way to the camp administration building. Once inside, Corrie was motioned to sit on a long wooden bench with nine other prisoners. An officer was sitting opposite them behind a large desk. He had piles of papers in front of him which he kept moving from side to side. Eventually, he looked up and called, "ten Boom, Cornelia, step up to the desk."

Corrie got painfully to her feet and shuffled over to his desk as she had been ordered.

"Birthday?" he asked.

Corrie had to think hard for a moment. "April 15, 1892," she finally replied.

"Good," the officer said as he pulled a large rubber stamp from the top drawer of his desk. He rubbed it on an ink pad several times and then thumped it down on the piece of paper in front of him. Then he handed the paper to Corrie and called the next name.

Corrie stepped back from the desk and stared at the paper. The rubber stamp had printed "Discharged" in red ink on the page. Could it possibly be true? After all she had been through, could she really be going home? Home to Nollie and Willem and the Beje? She looked around in wonder. Would this really be her last day in this terrible place?

"Follow me," commanded another guard, and Corrie was led into the next room. "Clothes over there. Final health check," said the guard, as she pointed to a pile of prison dresses on the floor. Corrie quickly took her clothes off and joined the group of naked women sitting at the far end of the room. They sat together and waited. Each of them held a piece of paper similar to Corrie's, but no one spoke. The women were all deep in their own thoughts. At first Corrie was thrilled to be free, but then she began to think the whole think might be a trap. Maybe they were really on their way to the gas chamber. She had heard that the Nazis played tricks like that so that prisoners would go quietly and unsuspectingly into the chamber.

"Through the door," motioned the guard.

All of a sudden Corrie could not move. She was too scared. What if there was a gas chamber on the other side of the door? Corrie saw panic on some of the other prisoners' faces. But since she had no choice but to obey, slowly she stood up and walked with the other women towards the door. To her relief, on the other side was a young man in a doctor's coat. "Stand against the wall," he told the women.

The women obeyed.

"Bend over. Touch your toes," he commanded. "Now, stand up straight," he barked, and then walked along the row of women. He looked each woman up and down. "Passed," he said three times; then he stopped at Corrie. He looked down and then said flatly, "Swollen legs. Hospital."

Corrie hurried along behind a trusty. "Is it true I've been released?" she asked.

The trusty looked at her kindly and said, "Yes. If you have the paper, you are released. But they won't let you go until you are well enough."

Corrie frowned.

The trusty went on, "The Nazis won't release prisoners who aren't healthy. They're scared it might look as though they didn't look after them properly."

Corrie nearly laughed out loud. She had been starved, beaten, and forced to work twelve hours a day, and every day in Ravensbruck, she had had to smell the burning bodies of women who had been gassed to death. And now they wouldn't release her because she had swollen legs! It made no sense at all.

The trusty led Corrie into the back of the hospital and spoke to the nurse. Corrie was given a top bunk against a wall. As she settled down on the bunk to think about the day's strange turn of events, she kept her legs propped up high against the wall. Swollen legs were the only thing that separated her from freedom!

Each morning Corrie got into a lineup of "released prisoners," and each morning the same thing was written on her paper: "Swollen legs, return for treatment." Corrie would return to her bunk and keep her legs elevated some more. The hospital had been a grim place when Betsie was brought to it, but now it had become a place of complete horror. A trainload of prisoners being transferred to Ravensbruck had been bombed by the Allies. Many of the women were badly hurt; some were missing arms and legs. The women screamed in agony through the night while the nurses mocked them and laughed at their pain. The bunks in the hospital were also so hopelessly overcrowded that during Corrie's first night there, four women rolled off the bunks to their death.

But Corrie decided that the women worst off in all of Ravensbruck were the women who lined up with her each morning for inspection. Like her, they knew they would be free to go if they just got well enough. But even Corrie could see some of them would never be well enough; they were yellow with jaundice or coughed up blood, a sure sign of tuberculosis. Corrie felt so sorry for them. How cruel it was for them to have freedom dangling just out of their reach.

Finally, on December 28, ten days after entering the hospital, Corrie heard the words she had been waiting to hear: "Passed inspection."

With those two words from the doctor, Corrie's whole world changed. Instead of returning to her bunk in the hospital or to Barracks 28, she was whisked through another set of doors and into a hallway. A trusty showed her into a small room where racks of recycled women's clothes hung in neat rows. "Find something that fits. I'll be back in a minute," said the trusty.

Corrie stared at the racks. Had she heard right? Did she get to choose for herself? She had been told what to do, where to sit, what to eat, and when to talk every day for the ten months she had been in prison, and now she was being told to choose for herself. She was still standing there when the trusty came back.

"Come on," said the trusty. "Let me help you."

Together they found a woolen skirt, a silk blouse, a hat and coat, and a good pair of lace-up shoes. Corrie had to leave the laces of the shoes undone, as her feet were still too swollen, but she tried to walk as if her feet were normal.

"There, you look wonderful," said the trusty as she led Corrie from the room to a desk where she was handed a pen.

"Sign this," said a guard, thrusting a piece of paper in front of her on the desk.

Corrie read what was written on the paper. It was a statement in German saying that the person signing had been treated well at Ravensbruck and had never been ill, never been hungry, and never been hurt. Her signature on the page was now all that stood between Corrie and freedom. Quickly she signed the paper.

Next she was given a slice of bread and a free train pass to get to the Dutch border. Last, a guard pulled a large manila envelope from a file cabinet and handed it to Corrie. With trembling hands, Corrie began to open the envelope. What could it possibly be? As she tore open the top of the envelope, out tumbled her mother's wedding ring, her gold watch, and the Dutch gilders she'd had in her dress pocket when the Gestapo raided the Beje. It seemed like a lifetime ago.

"Move along," said the guard, pointing towards the double doors at the end of the room. Corrie walked through them as she put on her wristwatch. She wound the watch and held it to her ear. It still ticked!

In the next room, she joined ten other women, all dressed in recycled clothes and clipping on watches, slipping on rings, and doing up necklaces. Corrie thought they looked like a bunch of ladies getting ready for church, except for one thing. They were all so thin that no matter how many clothes they had on, one could easily still see the outline of their bones.

Another guard walked in. "We are leaving," she announced as she swept through the room.

The women glanced at each other and then followed her out the door into the cold December morning. They followed her right up to the huge iron gates of Ravensbruck. The guard yelled a few words at the gatekeepers, and the gates swung open. Freedom! *Is it real, or was it a trick?* Corrie kept asking herself over and over as she walked through the gates, up over the rise, and down the railroad track to a small train station. As she sat at the station waiting for a train to arrive, a terrible thought struck her. She might be free, but was she any safer outside Ravensbruck than she had been inside? She was near Berlin, deep inside Germany, right in the middle of a war zone. How would she ever make it safely back to Holland?

Chapter 14

Out from Under the Grip

A train rumbled into the small station. It was a freight train, but that didn't matter to Corrie and the other women just released from Ravensbruck. They climbed into the empty boxcars. Corrie found herself sitting next to another Dutch woman, Claire Prins. As the train pulled away from the station, Corrie thought about the last time she'd ridden on a train. Eighty women to a car, no bathroom, and Betsie gasping for air. The memories flooded back, and soon tears were streaming down her face. Claire Prins, with her own memories and her own tears, put her arm around Corrie. "We are free, free at last," she said between sobs.

Corrie nodded and wiped her eyes. Betsie had been right. It was three days before New Year's Day

1945, and Corrie and Betsie, each in her own way, were free.

The train stopped many times, and as it did so, most of the other women from Ravensbruck got off to make connections. Finally, it was just Corrie and Claire alone in their boxcar. They peered out through the small holes in the sides of the car. Through them they could see the destruction of war. Hour after hour, the train chugged through burnt, barren countryside and cities inhabited by old people and women picking through the rubble of their homes. Corrie wondered what Haarlem would be like. Claire Prins, who had been sent to Ravensbruck from Holland after Corrie, told her that although southern Holland had been liberated by the Allied Forces, northern Holland was still in the grip of the Germans. The women were returning to Holland, but not a free Holland.

Finally, the train stopped one last time, and the boxcar door slid open. A man was standing by the door. "You women have to get out here. The train tracks have been blown up, and you can't go any farther by train," he said in perfect Dutch. Corrie and Claire smiled at each other; they were finally back in Holland.

Corrie and Claire climbed slowly from the boxcar and looked around. The train had stopped at a station. A sign on the platform read, "Welcome to Groningen." Groningen was in the very north of Holland. To get to Haarlem, Corrie still needed to travel across the country. She didn't know how she would do it, but nothing mattered more right then than being free and away from Germany.

A young woman on the platform looked at Corrie and Claire. "Excuse me," she said, "but you might find help at the Deaconess Hospital. It's about half a mile up the road."

Corrie thanked the woman, wondering how terrible they must look if a complete stranger felt it necessary to give them directions to a hospital! Slowly and painfully the two women made their way up the street until they finally collapsed into comfortable chairs in the hospital waiting room.

Within minutes, two nurses appeared. One asked Corrie to follow her, while Claire Prins went with the other. Corrie was led into a small office overlooking a garden covered with snow. Corrie could see the outlines of trees and bushes, which looked beautiful, even with snow covering them.

"Tell me about yourself," said the nurse, picking up a clipboard. "Where are you from?"

"Haarlem," replied Corrie.

The nurse broke into a smile. "I am from Haarlem, too. Did you know a Corrie ten Boom there?" inquired the nurse, and then she added, "she's probably quite a bit younger than you, I would think."

Corrie stared closely at the nurse. "Truus. Truus Benes! Yes, it is you."

"How did you know my name?" asked the nurse.

"It's me. I am Corrie ten Boom," said Corrie. "You were in my Triangle Club!"

"Tante Corrie. I don't believe it! Is it really you?" she asked in disbelief.

Corrie nodded, wondering again what she must look like to other people.

Corrie and Truus sat for half an hour while Corrie told her story. Truus ordered tea and a cookie for Corrie to eat while she talked.

"What would you like most of all?" Truus asked as Corrie finished her story.

Corrie replied straightaway. There was one thing she had not had for nearly eleven long months. "A hot bath," she said, longingly.

Soon Corrie was lying stretched out in a hot, deep bath. It felt so wonderful as the water lapped around her tired, aching body. But even more wonderful was the knowledge that no one was going to yell at her when she got out, and no one was going to escort her back to a barracks or cell.

Finally, after Truus had asked Corrie four times whether she wanted to get out, Corrie climbed from the tub and wrapped a clean, white towel around herself. How wonderful it felt! After Corrie dried herself, she decided to look in the mirror hanging on the left wall of the bathroom. She stood by the mirror for a moment, summoning her courage. Then she stepped in front of it and looked. Staring back at her was a scrawny old woman. Her hair was cut into short tufts, and her skin was deathly gray.

Truus Benes brought in a new set of clothes. Corrie was glad. She hadn't been able to stop wondering whether the clothes she'd been given at

Ravensbruck had belonged to some poor woman who had been gassed there. She was glad to be rid of anything that tied her thoughts to that horrible place.

Next, Corrie was taken to a private room, where she was given a bowl of soup and then tucked into bed. A bed with crisp white sheets, no less, and she had it all to herself. And no one was screaming in agony or cursing at her. She tried to stay awake for as long as possible to enjoy it all, but she was tired and was soon fast asleep.

When she finally awoke the next morning, breakfast was waiting, served on a white tablecloth with a silver knife and fork. Corrie could hardly believe the luxury.

Corrie stayed at the hospital for ten days. With rest and relaxation, the swelling in her legs quickly went down, and she felt much stronger after eating three meals a day. She also took a bath every day, and Nurse Benes arranged for her to have the little hair she had left "styled." But one problem remained—how was she to get back to Haarlem? The Germans had put a complete travel ban in place all over northern Holland. The only people who were able to travel about were those on official Nazi business. And while Corrie was being fed well in the hospital, all over Holland, people were starving. It was a particularly cold winter, and trees were being ripped out of the ground so that every last piece of them could be used for firewood. People were also chopping up furniture to burn and boiling their prized tulip bulbs to eat.

Dutch farmers in the north were forbidden by the Nazis to sell their produce in Holland. It was all supposed to go to Germany to keep the soldiers fighting, but many Dutch farmers found ways around the rule. One brave group was stealing food right off supply trains and trucking it south. News came to the hospital that if Corrie wanted to, she could ride in one of the trucks that was headed to Hilversum with a load of stolen produce.

Corrie's heart leapt at the opportunity. Hilversum was where Willem, Tine, and their children lived. On her eleventh night back in Holland, Corrie was ushered from the hospital into a large old truck. The truck lumbered through the backstreets of Groningen without its headlights on because it was too dangerous to use them.

Corrie prayed for a safe trip as the truck headed west. She knew they weren't supposed to be traveling, and at any moment the truck could be stopped by the Nazis. And if it were stopped, Corrie would be found riding in a truck loaded with stolen vegetables. She dared not think what would happen then. But she had to get home to Haarlem, and if this was the only way to do it, she was willing to risk being caught.

The truck drove on through the night and pulled to a halt in front of Willem's rest home just as the sun was beginning to rise. Willem's rest home looked just as it always had. Corrie climbed down from the cab of the truck and looked up the path that led to the front door. She stood for a moment and then slowly walked up the path towards the familiar brick building. As she approached the house, she remembered the last time she and Willem had both been free together. It had been nearly a year ago at the Beje when he was holding his weekly prayer meeting just as the Gestapo burst into the house. Corrie knocked loudly on the rest home door.

Within minutes, Willem, Tine, and their children excitedly surrounded Corrie, smothering her with hugs and kisses. They peppered her with questions, and as she told them about how Betsie had died in Ravensbruck, tears welled from their eyes. Then Tine reported how they had not heard anything from Kik since he had been taken to Germany. But the sadness was tempered by some good news. Willem told how all the people who had been hiding in the Beje, except Mary, had managed to avoid capture by the Nazis. And the underground network in Haarlem was still working hard hiding people from the Germans.

Corrie stayed the next week with Willem and his family, but by the second day with them, she realized Willem was ill. He did not like to talk about it, but Tine told Corrie that Willem had become sick with tuberculosis in jail and hadn't got any better after his release. Willem, though, carried on as if nothing had happened, working in the rest home and writing a book about the Old Testament. He also spent a lot of time figuring out how to get Corrie back to the Beje. He knew that she wouldn't feel completely at home until she was there.

At breakfast one day in late January, Willem announced that everything was set for Corrie to go back to the Beje. No trains were running, but a car would pick her up at eleven o'clock in the morning and take her there. Sure enough, at exactly 11:00 A.M., a black limousine pulled up in front of the rest home. The family waved good-bye as Corrie stepped into the limousine for the most luxurious drive of her life. She was curious how Willem had arranged such a wonderful ride, but she knew better than to ask. "Don't ask questions" was a lesson Corrie hadn't forgotten from her involvement in the underground.

The car zoomed towards Haarlem. No other vehicles were on the road, which gave the trip an eerie feeling. But with no traffic, in no time the limousine was turning at the corner past St. Bavo's Church into Barteljorisstraat. It rolled along the street and pulled to a halt in front of the clockshop. Corrie climbed out, and the car sped away. As it disappeared from view at the end of Barteljorisstraat, she took a deep breath. She had imagined this moment so many times, though always with Betsie standing beside her.

Before Corrie could open the door to the clockshop, it swung open, and Nollie rushed out. She enveloped Corrie with her arms. The two sisters hugged and clung to each other with tears of joy running down their cheeks. Finally, arm in arm they walked into the Beje. Waiting inside were Nollie's three daughters, who eagerly welcomed Tante Corrie home. The five of them walked together through the Beje. First, they went into Corrie's bedroom; the Angels' Den was still hidden behind the linen closet and bookcase. The Gestapo had never managed to discover the entrance to it. Next, they went into Tante Jans's old bedroom; the chair in which their mother had sat and looked out over Barteljorisstraat so many years before still sat by the window. In the kitchen, Betsie's favorite recipe book was still propped up beside the stove. And in the clockshop, Casper ten Boom's eyeglass lay on his workbench, right where he had left it. All the things were still there in the Beje, but the people who made it home were not. As Corrie walked through the house, both happiness and sadness mingled inside her. Corrie was happy to be free, happy to be back in Haarlem in the Beje, but sad because Betsie and her father were not there and would never be there again.

Together Nollie, Corrie, and the girls cleaned the house until it was spotless. But somehow, after all the dreams and longing to be back at the Beje, it didn't feel like home to Corrie anymore. Even after she resumed her watchmaking career, she would sit down to replace the mainspring in a watch and not be able to concentrate on the task. All the time she felt as though she should be somewhere else doing something else.

Despite what she was feeling, throughout the spring of 1945, Corrie tried hard to pick up and go on with her life as it had been before the Gestapo raid. But her attempt to get back to normal was made even more difficult by the fact that northern Holland was still under German occupation. Hitler had pulled all his occupying troops out of Norway, Denmark, Belgium, and France, but for whatever reason, he was unwilling to loosen his grip on northern Holland. This left the citizens of Haarlem and other northern towns in a terrible situation. They had no food, no fuel, and no transportation. Dutch citizens were dying from starvation and the cold right in their own homes, while in many other parts of Europe, people were celebrating their liberation from German occupation.

Spring dragged on, and Corrie watched as so many people she knew became desperate to survive, almost as desperate as the prisoners she and Betsie had been with in Vught and Ravensbruck concentration camps. As she saw what was happening to them, she remembered Betsie's words: "We must tell the people there is no pit so deep that God's love is not deeper." As she recalled those words, Corrie knew what was missing from her life. She wasn't supposed to be in the clockshop repairing watches. God wanted her out telling these desperate people about His love for them.

Within days, Corrie had begun speaking in homes and at church gatherings. It was difficult for her to relive the pain she had been through, but the stories she told about herself and Betsie gave many people courage to go on. And because of that, despite her emotional pain, Corrie knew she could not stop speaking about her experience.

Then on May 1, 1945, news quickly buzzed through Holland that Adolf Hitler was dead. The official word was that he had died fighting the enemy. The world would later learn he had committed suicide in a bunker in Berlin.

All Holland held its breath. Surely it was only a matter of days now before the Nazis surrendered and gave up Holland. And it was. On Tuesday, May 8, 1945, Canadian tanks rolled into Haarlem. The bells of St. Bavo's Church rang out, and everyone crowded into the streets.

Corrie had one thing to do before she joined the others in the street. She took her father's portrait off the wall in the parlor and carried it down to the clockshop. Lovingly she set it in the front window of the shop. Then she climbed the stairs again and brought down the old family Bible that he had read from every morning and evening. She opened it at Psalm 91 and laid it in the window. Then she took orange (the Dutch royal color) ribbons and draped them across Casper ten Boom's portrait. "Now," Corrie said to herself, "he too is a part of this great day." With that she slipped out the side door of the Beje and disappeared into the throng of celebrating Dutch people, free Dutch people, who were finally out from under the clutches of Nazi Germany.

Chapter 15

Help, Hope, and Healing

Even though the war was over, things did not return to normal in Holland. The whole Dutch way of life had been damaged. Almost every family in the country was missing a son or a nephew. And for the ten Boom family, their nightmare did not immediately end with the war. In 1946, Willem ten Boom died, having never fully recovered from the tuberculosis he contracted while imprisoned by the Nazis. He died without knowing what had happened to his oldest son, Kik. It wasn't until several years later that Tine finally learned that their son had died in the Bergen-Belsen concentration camp in Germany.

Slowly, information began to come out about how brutal and terrible Adolf Hitler and the Nazis had really been. It was worse than anyone had imagined. Of the 115,000 Jews in Holland before the war, only about 8,500 had survived. And throughout Europe, between eighteen million and twenty-six million people had died in concentration camps. It was hard to get an exact number because so many people had just disappeared with no trace. But two numbers that were known were that at least six million Jews and four hundred thousand Gypsies had been killed. Some of the pictures photographers took of what the Allies found when they entered the concentration camps were so horrible that they were never published. When all the soldiers killed were added in, the Second World War claimed over fifty million lives and destroyed some of the world's most beautiful cities.

Before he died, Willem was able to locate the unmarked grave in Scheveningen where Casper ten Boom had been buried. The ten Boom family had his body reburied in the war cemetery at Loenen, along with hundreds of other brave men and women who, working for the underground, had given their lives for their fellow countrymen. The "Grand Old Man" of Haarlem finally had the resting place he deserved. Corrie wept during the dedication service of his new grave. She mourned that Betsie's body would never lie beside his.

Corrie stayed busy speaking after the war. More than ever, people needed to hear about how to forgive others and go on with their lives. She was especially concerned for the people who, like her, had been held captive by the Nazis and had witnessed unspeakable horrors. Many of them had been so terrified by what they saw and experienced that they found it hard to fit into normal life.

During this time, there was one particular meeting Corrie spoke at that she never forgot. It was like many of the other meetings, until the end, when a well-dressed woman came up to her.

"Hello," said the woman. "I am Mrs. Bierens de Haan, and I live in Bloemendaal."

Corrie nodded. She knew the area well. Years before she had regularly taken her Walking Club for strolls around the gardens of the palatial homes there.

"Do you still live in that little house with the clockshop downstairs?" asked Mrs. de Haan kindly.

Corrie frowned, wondering whether she should know this woman. "Yes, I do," she replied. "How do you know about it?"

Mrs. de Haan smiled. "My mother used to tell me stories about her visits there. She would go to visit a woman who had been married to a pastor."

Corrie smiled. "Tante Jans. She was always involving ladies in charity work."

Mrs. de Haan nodded. "Yes, my mother was very interested in charity, and so am I. When you were speaking about the need for a place for those released from Nazi prisons and concentration camps to go to recuperate, I had the strangest impression that I should talk to you. My husband is dead, but we had five sons together. All five of them worked in the underground, and one of them, Jan, was captured and taken off to Germany. We have not heard a word from him since."

"So you want me to pray for him, Mrs. de Haan? I would be honored to do that," said Corrie, trying to anticipate where Mrs. de Haan was headed with the conversation.

"No, that's not it," she said with a smile. "When I was listening to you, I felt God tell me two things. First, Jan would be fine and coming home soon, and second, when he comes home I should hand my home over to you for your work as a way of saying thank you."

For a moment Corrie didn't know what to say. It sounded like Mrs. de Haan thought she had made some sort of a bargain with God to get her son back. Corrie did not want to be a part of that. What if her son didn't come home? Not many underground workers who were captured did. Quickly she tried to think of some way to let Mrs. de Haan down gently.

"That's very kind of you," Corrie began, "but back in Ravensbruck, shortly before she died, Betsie described to me the inside of a home. She was very specific about the details, and I believe in her memory I should do my best to find a home like the one she described." Corrie paused to recall Betsie's description. "The house she described had inlaid wood floors, and there were marble statues set in little nooks all along the walls. And the staircase was wide, and the windows were tall and went all the way to the ceiling...."

Corrie stopped midsentence when she saw the beaming smile that had spread across Mrs. de Haan's face.

"Then that settles it," said Mrs. de Haan. "I see you've been to my house already. I can't wait for Jan to get home!"

Corrie was amazed by her reply, but not nearly as amazed as when Mrs. de Haan's son Jan returned home alive and well a few days later. And nothing compared to how amazed she was when later that week she toured the de Haan home. It was exactly like the house Betsie had described to her in Ravensbruck. Corrie had thought that in her delirious mind Betsie may have been describing what she thought heaven was like, but in fact she had been describing the inside of Mrs. de Haan's home. It gave Corrie goosebumps to walk across the inlaid wood floor and stare up at the statues set into nooks in the walls. It was a beautiful place, a perfect place for people to rest and get over the trauma of being held captive in a concentration camp.

True to her word, Mrs. de Haan handed over the fifty-six-room home to Corrie. Within a month, the house was filled with people. Some of them were newly released from concentration camps. Some were Jews who had spent the past five years hiding in attics and cellars. Others were Dutch people who had been bombed out of their homes and had nowhere else to go. Still others were orphans whose entire families had been wiped out by the Nazis.

Many people came to help Corrie with her work. Doctors and nurses, gardeners and house-keepers, all came to lend a hand. But many who came to help thought that Corrie should run the home more strictly. For example, at three o'clock every morning, one man got up and walked to Haarlem. He had spent a good part of the war in a concentration camp, and Corrie knew he needed to know he was free to go anywhere at any time. Some people thought the gates should be locked at night so he could not go out. Corrie, though, refused to lock anything. She had seen enough locks and barbed wire to last a lifetime, and so had many of the people who came to her for help at the de Haan house.

Meals, too, were served anytime anyone wanted something to eat. Again, some nurses suggested that Corrie have bells and proper mealtimes, but Corrie could not do it. The lives of the people she was helping had been entirely regulated by horns and bells for so long that they, like her, never wanted to hear either again. Corrie remembered how wonderful it had been when she got to the hospital at Groningen. She remembered the smell of the fresh sheets, the kindness of the nurses, the Bach music playing on the radio, and the shelves stocked with books. Kindness and beauty, they were the things the survivors needed most of all, and Corrie did all she could to provide them for the people who came to her for help.

Many people found healing and peace at the de Haan home, but one group of people could find no peace anywhere in Holland. It seemed no one wanted to help them. They were the men and women who had been a part of the National Socialist Bond (NSB), which had helped the Nazis control Holland. As soon as the war was over, their neighbors turned on them, showing all the anger and hatred they had not been allowed to express for five years. The members of the NSB were thrown out of their homes and spat upon when they went out in public. Corrie felt sorry for them and invited several to live in the de Haan house in Bloemendaal. This turned out to be a disaster. The people who had lost family members and friends because members of the NSB had betrayed them would not welcome them into the house. There were huge arguments, and in the end, Corrie had to give up the idea of forcing them to live together.

Corrie came up with another idea, however. She remembered the night her father had been arrested and his words to the Nazi official who had offered him his freedom. "Tomorrow morning I will open my doors again to anyone who is in need of my help," he had said to the officer. Casper ten Boom would have let members of the NSB into his home; Corrie was sure of it. So in honor of him, she allowed those who had been in the National Socialist

Bond to take over the Beje and live in it. Six or seven of them at a time went to live in the home of a man whom a member of the group had betrayed. There they found help and healing.

Gradually the people at Bloemendaal followed Corrie's example and began to reach out to their fellow countrymen and women living at the Beje. But as she was urging people to forgive others, especially those who had been members of the NSB, Corrie was wrestling with her own thoughts and feelings. An old friend from the underground had told her where Jan Vogel was living. Jan Vogel was the man who had visited her the night before the raid, asking for six hundred guilders. Corrie knew she had to forgive him. Finally, one day, she felt strong enough to get out a pen and paper and begin writing him a letter. "I heard that you are most likely the person who betrayed my family and me. As a result, I was in a concentration camp for ten months. My father died in prison nine days after he was arrested. My sister died in Ravensbruck concentration camp...."

Corrie struggled to write the letter. "God, I do not have the strength to forgive this man; please give me Your strength," she prayed as she wrote. Eventually, she finished the letter, telling Jan Vogel she forgave him for the terrible thing he had done to the ten Boom family and urging him to ask God to forgive him also.

By 1947, so many people wanted to help with the work at the de Haan house in Bloemendaal that

Corrie had time to write and travel. It was during this time she wrote her first book, *A Prisoner and Yet....* Most of the book was written in the early hours of the morning. Two years after being released from Ravensbruck, Corrie still awoke at 4:30 every morning, the time the prisoners had gotten up for roll call. The book told the story of Corrie and Betsie's time at Vught and Ravensbruck. The message of the book was that God wants all persons to forgive those who have wronged them. After writing the difficult letter to Jan Vogel forgiving him, Corrie thought she was living the message of her book, that is, until she traveled to Germany to speak.

At a large church in Munich, she spoke about how God asks people to forgive one another and how, with His love, they can become like brothers and sisters, no matter what their nationality. When Corrie had finished speaking, many people came up to thank her for what she had said. She shook their hands and thanked them for coming and listening. Then, when the church was nearly empty, Corrie spotted a tall man with blond hair making his way towards her. In a flash she was back in the shower building at Ravensbruck. This man, an SS Guard, was standing by the door, hand on his gun, leering at the women prisoners as he made them strip. Corrie stood motionless as he approached her. She heard his voice as if it were a million miles away. "Thank you for your talk," he said. "It is so wonderful to know God forgives all our sins, isn't it?"

Corrie looked at the man standing in front of her. Instead of seeing his smiling face, she saw the faces of Betsie and her father. The man thrust out his hand to shake Corrie's, and as he did so, hatred filled her heart. She would not and could not lift her hand to shake his.

"Oh God," she prayed silently, "help me to live my message."

As she prayed those words, it was as though a strong jolt of electricity had run through her body. Her arm stretched out as though she had no control over it, and she shook the man's hand. As she did so, all the hatred she felt melted away, and she knew she had forgiven him.

"Yes, it is wonderful to know that God forgives all our sins!" she said, meaning every word.

Later, in Germany, another man came to see Corrie. He had heard about the work at the de Haan house in Bloemendaal. He was a member of the German Lutheran Church, and he told Corrie that the new German government wanted the church to open a similar home for Germans who had been devastated by the war and were still struggling to adapt to normal life. He asked Corrie if she would help to set it up. Corrie thought it was a good idea, until she heard where it was going to be located—in a former concentration camp called Darmstadt. She didn't think she had the strength to go inside another concentration camp, even though it had been closed for two years, much less turn it into a place of recovery. However, Betsie's words rang in her mind: "We must tell them there is no pit so deep that God's love is not deeper." Despite her feelings, Corrie knew what she had to do, and she set about turning Darmstadt into a place of hope and healing.

The years sped by for Corrie. In 1953, Nollie died, leaving Corrie feeling very alone. Corrie was the last of Casper ten Boom's children still alive. But she did not give up her work. More opportunities came for her to speak and share her simple message. All in all, she visited over sixty countries, including Cuba, Taiwan, Israel, and New Zealand. In 1956, she went on one of her speaking trips with Dr. Bob Pierce, founder of World Vision. They had just finished a series of meetings in Taiwan when he made a ridiculous suggestion. "Why don't you meet with Queen Wilhelmina of the Netherlands?"

Corrie laughed. She decided that since Bob Pierce was an American, he didn't understand that a Dutch commoner did not make an appointment to see the Queen.

"It's not that easy," she told him.

"Well," replied Bob Pierce, "pray about it and see what happens."

Corrie agreed to do that, but she knew she had done nothing extraordinary in Holland. Many thousands of Dutch people had been as brave as she had been, and some had suffered far more than she had suffered. Still, she would pray about it.

When Corrie got back to the Netherlands, she sent a letter to Wilhelmina, who now called herself

Princess Wilhelmina because she had stepped aside from the throne so that her daughter Juliana could become queen. Three days later, the royal car was outside Corrie's house waiting to pick Corrie up. Corrie sat in shock all the way to "'t Loo," where the royal palace was located. Corrie and Princess Wilhelmina became good friends, and the princess invited Corrie back for many evening chats. Corrie told her all about her life and how God had given her a message of forgiveness to take to the world. She also told Princess Wilhelmina about her father and how he had prayed for her every morning of his life—how he would have loved to know that his youngest daughter actually sat in the palace and talked with Wilhelmina about God's love!

As Corrie got older, she found it more difficult to travel alone, so she was joined by an assistant, Conny van Hoogstraten. Together they continued traveling the world, where Corrie would share her message with anyone who would listen.

On one of her trips to the United States, Corrie met a talented writing duo, John and Elizabeth Sherrill, who listened to her story and read her book *A Prisoner and Yet....* The Sherrills asked Corrie if they could work with her on a book that would tell the whole story of the ten Boom family during the German occupation of Holland. Corrie agreed, and in 1971, *The Hiding Place* was published.

The book was an instant hit, selling over two million copies. Suddenly, Corrie ten Boom was a well-known figure to Christians around the world.

Although she found it difficult being famous, she was grateful that the fame helped to spread her message even farther afield. Wherever she went, she took a box of her books to give away to people, all sorts of people. At an airport, she would start a conversation with a skycap. "I bet you really know your way through this airport," she would comment. The skycap would agree, proud that someone had noticed. "Well, that is wonderful," Corrie would go on. "But it is more important that you know the way to heaven. Do you?" Then she would pull out one of her books, sign it, and hand it to the skycap with great flourish. "Here, read this, and if you have any questions, write to me." She would tuck an address card into the book.

When she had settled into her seat on the airplane, she would stop a stewardess. "Would you please give this to the pilot?" she would ask as she handed the stewardess two copies of her book, one for her to keep and one for the pilot.

From the time *The Hiding Place* was published, Corrie was hardly ever back in Holland. She slept in a different bed almost every night as she busily kept up her travel schedule. However, in 1974, she got to return to Haarlem. *The Hiding Place* was being turned into a movie, which was filming in Holland.

Corrie took the cast and crew of the movie to visit the Beje. She led them along Barteljorisstraat and up to the familiar green door of the Beje. She opened the door and stepped back in time. The Beje was still filled with memories of her mother and father and Betsie. As she ushered the cast and crew inside, she stopped in her tracks. The was a noise coming from upstairs. She motioned for the others to stay put downstairs while she climbed the stairs to investigate. The noise grew louder and louder as she climbed. It was coming from her old bedroom on the third floor, and it was the sound of Hebrew chanting. Loud, sorrowful chanting. Corrie knew the voice could belong to only one person, Eusie!

She tiptoed to the door of her old bedroom and peeked in. There, side by side, stood Eusie and Hans Poley. Eusie was chanting, and Hans was listening with his eyes closed. When they had finished, Corrie walked into the room. All three of them embraced warmly.

"What are you doing here?" she finally asked.

"It has been thirty years since we were hiding here," said Eusie, waving his hand towards the Angels' Den. "When we sat in there hour after hour wondering whether we would be caught by the Nazis, I made a promise to God. I told Him that if I got out alive, I would come back to this place to sing praises to Him in my loudest voice. Not only did I make it through, but my wife and three children also survived. We are the only Jewish family I know who survived the war intact." His voice cracked, and then he went on, "Today I came back to sing."

Corrie smiled. Her father would have loved to hear the Jewish cantor's voice resounding through the Beje once more.

Finally, the three of them descended the stairs. In the clockshop, the cast and crew were waiting eagerly for a report on the noise upstairs. Corrie introduced Eusie and Hans to the cast, who peppered them both with questions about their experiences hiding out in the Beje during the war.

Corrie continued to travel the globe, sharing her message of love and forgiveness. Occasionally, she would feel it was time for her to settle down and lead a quiet life, but then she would remember Betsie's words: "We must tell them there is no pit so deep that God's love is not deeper." Whenever Corrie heard those words ring in her mind, she knew she had to keep going.

In 1976, at the age of eighty-four, Corrie was still going strong. She and her assistant embarked on an eighteen-city tour of the United States that took seven months. Eventually, though, Billy Graham, who had befriended Corrie, convinced her she should settle down a little and stop her hectic pace, which would wear a woman half her age out! So in 1977, Corrie and her new assistant, Pam Rosewell, moved into a ranch-style house in the suburb of Placentia located in Orange County, California. Corrie might have agreed to stay put in one place, but she hadn't said anything about stopping! She announced to Pam her latest plan. She would produce five new books and five new teaching movies in less than two years.

By her eighty-seventh birthday, Corrie had completed her plan. But the effort and energy required to do it had taken its toll on her body. One morning soon afterwards, Corrie awoke to find she could not move at all. Lying in bed, she knew what had happened. She had suffered a massive stroke, just as her mother had sixty years before. At first, everyone thought Corrie was going to die, but she didn't. She recovered a little, but she could no longer speak. Then she had a second and a third stroke. Her old Dutch friend Lotte Reimeringer moved into the house to help Pam Rosewell take care of her. They played the music of Bach and Beethoven on the stereo and took turns reading to Corrie. They even read some of her own books to her. As they read, Corrie relived her happy childhood with Betsie, Willem, and Nollie. She could hear Peter's wonderful organ music and see her mother doing embroidery. She remembered her father sitting in his favorite chair and experienced again the joy of running through the sand dunes with her Triangle Club girls. And she would smile and nod. What a wonderful life she had lived. Her experiences had made her famous, and her books and movies would have made her rich if she hadn't given nearly all her money away to various causes.

Corrie had faithfully followed the encouragement Betsie had given her thirty-three years before. She had spent the rest of her life after being released from Ravensbruck telling people there was no pit so deep that God's love wasn't deeper. Finally, the woman who had lived to tell others about love and forgiveness died quietly in her bed on April 15, 1983, on her ninety-first birthday.

Corrie ten Boom was buried in Los Angeles, and her gravestone was inscribed, "Corrie ten Boom, 1892–1983, Jesus is Victor."

ten Boom, Corrie. *In My Father's House*. Fleming H. Revell Company, 1976.

ten Boom, Corrie. *Prison Letters*. Fleming H. Revell Company, 1975.

ten Boom, Corrie, with Jamie Buckingham. *Tramp for the Lord*. Fleming H. Revell Company, 1974.

ten Boom, Corrie, with John and Elizabeth Sherrill. *The Hiding Place*. Fleming H. Revell Company, 1971.

Poley, Hans. *Return to the Hiding Place*. Chariot Family Publishing, 1993.

Rosewell, Pamela. *The Five Silent Years of Corrie ten Boom*. Zondervan Publishing House, 1986.

Wellman, Sam. *Corrie ten Boom: Heroine of Haarlem*. Barbour and Company, 1985.

White, Kathleen. *Corrie ten Boom*. Bethany House Publishers, 1983.

Janet and Geoff Benge are a husband and wife writing team with twenty years of writing experience. Janet is a former elementary school teacher. Geoff holds a degree in history. Originally from New Zealand, the Benges spent ten years serving with Youth With A Mission. They have two daughters, Laura and Shannon, and an adopted son, Lito. They make their home in the Orlando, Florida, area.

Also from Janet and Geoff Benge...

More adventure-filled biographies for ages 10 to 100!

Christian Heroes: Then & Now

Another exciting series from Janet and Geoff Benge!

Heroes of History

Also available:

Unit Study Curriculum Guides

Turn a great reading experience into an even greater
learning opportunity with a Unit Study Curriculum Guide.
Available for select Christian Heroes: Then & Now
and Heroes of History biographies.

Heroes for Young Readers

Written by Renee Taft Meloche • Illustrated by Bryan Pollard

Introduce younger children to the lives of these heroes with
rhyming text and captivating color illustrations!

**All of these series are available from YWAM Publishing
1-800-922-2143 / www.ywampublishing.com**